'This comprehensive book explains the complex and critical issues of early years safeguarding sensitively and in-depth. Rachel's knowledge, insights and first-hand experiences are evident throughout the book, especially in the Reflective sections. The breadth of content makes it an ideal resource for both the designated safeguarding lead and anyone else working directly with children and their families. I would highly recommend it as compulsory reading for everyone in the early years sector.'

– **Kathy Brodie**, *Founder of Early Years TV and the Early Years Summit*

'This excellent book provides early years professionals with everything they need to know about child protection and safeguarding in the early years. As with Rachel's training delivery, her writing style makes the content accessible to all, understandable, informative and easy to translate to practice. At Thrive Childcare we have been in receipt of Rachel's Child Protection and Safeguarding training for many years now, across both England and Scotland, and I cannot recommend this book enough.'

– **Ursula Krystek-Walton**, *Head of Early Years Thrive Childcare and Education*

'This book will be hugely welcomed by early years leaders and practitioners alike. It is highly relevant and insightful, whilst being really accessible and straightforward, fulfilling a real need in the sector.

Its content is validating for those carrying out the really tough job of safeguarding children in early years settings. Rachel has drawn on her extensive personal experience to create a reference book as well as a guidebook for DSLs and practitioners, providing regular reflection points for readers.

The book covers critical concepts such as professional curiosity, and wariness of inappropriate optimism to name just a couple. She reminds us about self-care and the importance of taking action and critically that safeguarding knowledge is about keeping children safe, not keeping Ofsted happy!'

– **Jo Kinloch**, *Managing Director, Mulberry Bush Nursery Group*

'I've had the privilege to have known Rachel for over 20 years. She has provided training and support to our local childminder networks and to many childminders personally, me included. Rachel has always been such a wonderful advocate for childminders, and this continues to be a strong feature in this brilliant book which highlights the challenges and experiences of many of us working to safeguard and protect children. The book recognises the real issues which are often difficult and hard to work around but Rachel acknowledges this and offers useful and helpful strategies for childminders to engage with and apply in practice. This book will be a real game changer. It simplifies a difficult subject; it reminds us of how vital our roles as childminders are when working with children and families and it challenges us to build upon what we already know and do. I can't wait to use it for training in my own team.'

– **Charlotte Cassidy**, *Childminder, Bury*

'This book is second to none in terms of its breadth and depth of what remains a deeply complex and ever-evolving subject. Rachel Buckler's expertise shines through in each of the seven chapters, providing information that is accessible and pertinent – and directly applicable to child care practitioners. She prioritises the empowerment of practitioners through equipping them with the diverse strategies provided throughout the book, as well as through broaching subjects that some might find it difficult to think about – let alone talk about and most importantly act on – when it comes to safeguarding and protecting children.'

– **Dr Mine Conkbayir**, *Early Years author, trainer and researcher*

Developing Child-Centred Practice for Safeguarding and Child Protection

Placing children at the centre of safeguarding principles and practices is vital for ensuring the best child protection. This essential resource provides early years practitioners with all that they need to be confident and competent as they fulfil their roles and obligations to safeguard and protect children.

Exploring the main factors that impact on the lives of young children in the current safeguarding climate, this book is a starting point for understanding the risks and categories of abuse and neglect. Grounded in best practice, it gives practitioners encouragement and advice to help shape and drive practice forward with child-centred motives, practices and perspectives.

The book offers:

- Insights into the current safeguarding climate backed by practical examples.
- An introduction to managing the different safeguarding challenges faced by early years professionals.
- Methods for contextualising these for children in the early years.
- Guidance on supporting vulnerable children, their families and other agencies working alongside them.
- Reflections, case studies and a wide range of example scenarios.
- Voices and insights from across the sector woven throughout for a holistic understanding of safeguarding.

With accessible chapters drawing on best practice from across the sector at every level, this is a valuable resource for all those working in the early years, whether just starting out or highly experienced in the field.

Rachel Buckler is a highly experienced practitioner, trainer and consultant working in support of safeguarding and child protection practices. During her 30-year career in children's service social care, she has developed and managed services including Sure Start Children's Centres and been a strategic lead for early intervention services delivered in Greater Manchester. Rachel continues to deliver training to local authorities' early years workforces, as well as providing training and consultancy for independent nurseries and childcare providers across the country. Rachel is co-founder of the Early Years Hub and creator of the Safeguarding Hub.

This book is dedicated to my Mom, Hilda, who was with me when I began to write but sadly didn't see me complete it. I know she would have liked it! And for Theo and Grace, the latest arrivals in our family.

Little Minds Matter:

Promoting Social and Emotional Wellbeing in the Early Years

Series Advisor: Sonia Mainstone-Cotton

The *Little Minds Matter* series promotes best practice for integrating social and emotional health and wellbeing into the early years setting. It introduces practitioners to a wealth of activities and resources to support them in each key area: from providing access to ideas for unstructured, imaginative outdoor play; activities to create a sense of belonging and form positive identities; and, importantly, strategies to encourage early years professionals to create a workplace that positively contributes to their own wellbeing, as well as the quality of their provision. The *Little Minds Matter* series ensures that practitioners have the tools they need to support every child.

Outdoor Play for Healthy Little Minds
Practical Ideas to Promote Children's Wellbeing in the Early Years
Sarah Watkins

Supporting the Wellbeing of Children with SEND
Essential Ideas for Early Years Educators
Kerry Payne

Supporting Behaviour and Emotions in the Early Years
Strategies and Ideas for Early Years Educators
Tamsin Grimmer

A Guide to Mental Health for Early Years Educators
Putting Wellbeing at the Heart of Your Philosophy and Practice
Kate Moxley

Supporting the Wellbeing of Children with EAL
Essential Ideas for Practice and Reflection
Liam Murphy

Building Positive Relationships in the Early Years
Conversations to Empower Children, Professionals, Families and Communities
Sonia Mainstone-Cotton and Jamel Carly Campbell

Developing Child-Centred Practice for Safeguarding and Child Protection
Strategies for Every Early Years Setting
Rachel Buckler

Little Brains Matter
A Practical Guide to Brain Development and Neuroscience in Early Childhood
Debbie Garvey

Developing Child-Centred Practice for Safeguarding and Child Protection

Strategies for Every Early Years Setting

Rachel Buckler

Routledge
Taylor & Francis Group

LONDON AND NEW YORK

Designed cover image: Me and my friend by Hiro

First published 2023
by Routledge
4 Park Square, Milton Park, Abingdon, Oxon OX14 4RN

and by Routledge
605 Third Avenue, New York, NY 10158

Routledge is an imprint of the Taylor & Francis Group, an informa business

© 2023 Rachel Buckler

The right of Rachel Buckler to be identified as author of this work has been asserted in accordance with sections 77 and 78 of the Copyright, Designs and Patents Act 1988.

British Library Cataloguing-in-Publication Data
A catalogue record for this book is available from the British Library

ISBN: 978-0-367-68347-4 (hbk)
ISBN: 978-0-367-68349-8 (pbk)
ISBN: 978-1-003-13705-4 (ebk)

DOI: 10.4324/9781003137054

Typeset in Optima
by Apex CoVantage, LLC

Contents

Acknowledgements

Writing this book has been a journey of past recollections, reflections and, in turn, renewed appreciation for all practitioners working with children to keep them safe and well. What an incredible achievement and difference you are making in the lives of our youngest of children.

Thank you to those who provided case studies and examples of best practice showcasing their strategies, learning, challenges and experiences when developing child-centred practices for safeguarding and child protection in the early years.

Special thanks for their contributions go to:

Sunflower Nursery Group, Tameside
Portico Nursery Group, Northwest
Thatto Heath Playdays, St Helens
Next Generation Nursery, Wigan
Honey Bears Nursery, Wigan
KidzRus Nursery Group, Salford
Kath Portlock – Childminder, Bury
Tricia Pritchard, Lizzie Watts, Christina Saitos and Pauline Daniel, formerly of the British Association of Professional Nannies (BAPN)
Liz Williams, Andrea Rusollo and staff from Victoria Family Centre, Bury
Rafik Idin, Independent Safeguarding Social Work Consultant
Marie McKittrick, Registered General Nursery (RGN) and former school nurse

Dr Mine Conkbayir, for her inspirational and ground breaking work in neuroscience and trauma informed practice. Her contributions to my own learning and indeed this book have been invaluable.

A big thank you to Mei and Hiro Wantanbe and Ivy Hawnt for allowing me to share their wonderful artwork within the book.

I also want to recognise and send appreciation to the many early years practitioners from my hometown of Bury, Greater Manchester with whom I have had the privilege to work with and share such valuable learning with over a number of years.

Recognition and thanks go to Pete and Louise Crolla, I would not be writing this book if they had not encouraged me to develop safeguarding and child protection training for our Early Years Hub all those years ago.

Finally, to my numerous friends and ex-colleagues working so incredibly hard in front line children's services, working tirelessly and passionately to make a difference for all children whilst empowering a children's workforce to do likewise. Thank you especially to Sue Myers, my good friend and inadvertent mentor, who is a true inspiration, ground breaker and shaker in the work of child protection, and to Mawuli Amesu, who provides me with ongoing expert guidance, reflection and professional supervision.

Foreword

This latest book in the Little Minds Matter series is on the vital subject of safeguarding and child protection. We know this is an essential part of our work, one that we all need to stay up to date with and has to be the foundation of all our practice. In this book Rachel brings a wealth of experience and knowledge in an accessible, reflective and encouraging way. I am so grateful to Rachel for writing this book for our series; it is challenging subject, but one that she supports us to understand and feel equipped to make a difference.

In this book, Rachel unpicks and explains the many aspects of safeguarding and child protection. She recognises it is a heavy subject, and weaves throughout the book tips about supporting staff and our own well-being. Through her writing, Rachel helps us feel supported in our learning with her gently and expertly guiding us though the area. She shares stories from her own and others' practice, and case studies and reflective questions weave throughout, giving us space to think about what we have read and our practice.

Rachel offers us a comprehensive guide to safeguarding and child protection; it is one that we can all use and learn from and I believe this book is one that every setting should have. It is a book you can use as a regular part of team development, it is a book that individuals can dip in and out of, and a book to use as part of the induction process for new staff. I think it will also become an important text for childcare and early years courses. I know it is book I will keep returning to and will be encouraging all the settings I work with to have a copy.

Sonia Mainstone-Cotton
Series Advisor
July 2022

Preface
A letter for every early years practitioner

Dear early years practitioner,

Firstly, I want to thank you for taking time to read this book. Whether you are a seasoned early years practitioner or if you are just setting out on your journey, preparing to navigate your way around the world of safeguarding and child protection, this book is for you. If you work in a large organisation, have leadership responsibilities for multiple settings, or support children in a playgroup, nursery or out of school provision, this book is for you too. If you lead a group, work in a team, are a student, a volunteer or a childminder's assistant, or operate independently as a lone childminder or nanny, this book is for you also. You see it doesn't really matter what our roles are when considering child-centred safeguarding practice, the common theme at the heart of our practice will always centre on children and achieve what is in their best interests.

When I was asked to write this book, I was excited to work with the remit that it would be applicable to 'every early years practitioner'. I hope that you can recognise my numerous acknowledgements of the important and vital work delivered through the early years sector by skilled and determined practitioners engaging in effective safeguarding and child protection strategies and practices. I also hope that as you work through each chapter you can consider your practice in light of refreshed and maybe new knowledge and concepts. Most importantly, you the reader will be able to apply the content in terms of what this means to you, your own setting and for the children you are working with. I have provided lots of opportunities to reflect and think about practice as independent learners and as part of your wider team if you are working with others.

Safeguarding and child protection can often be one of the most challenging aspects of early years practice. My encouragement to you is to continually invest in ways that enable you to learn and develop as a competent and confident practitioner and I hope that by reading this book it will contribute some way in helping you to achieve this.

*Please be aware that an element of content in this book proves a difficult read and may trigger emotional responses for some. If you find any of the content upsetting, please speak to someone who can support you. This may be a colleague, a line manager or someone outside of your workplace. One such organisation that support adults' recovery from childhood abuse is the **National Association for People Abused in Childhood (NAPAC);** they can be contacted on 0808 801 0331 or via their website at http://napac.org.uk

Yours,
Rachel Buckler

Safeguarding and child protection practice in the early years

Part one: working in the early years

Early years practitioners provide such a vital role in safeguarding and protecting young children. It almost goes without saying but there are lots of reasons as to why this is so. The work undertaken by childminders, nurseries, pre-schools, and other early years professionals, provide children with the help, protection and support that they need. These early interventions have the potential to contribute to positive outcomes at the most important stage in a child's life from the age of birth to five.

To put some of this into context this first chapter will explore some of the reasons why there is such a need to help and protect young children and why it is so important to put their needs and wellbeing at the heart of all that we do in the early years. We will also consider the reasons why and how the early years workforce is so well placed to provide appropriate responses in such a unique and effective way. Furthermore, we will acknowledge the challenges and obstacles that present to early years professionals. These challenges often require smart navigation and resolve delivered by a skilled and determined workforce.

Children under five – vulnerabilities and risks

A study researching child protection referrals in England found that one in five children were referred to children's services and one in nineteen were investigated before they reached the age of five. The study, undertaken by Bilson and Martin (2017), concluded some startling statistics.

DOI: 10.4324/9781003137054-1

Before a child's fifth birthday,

- 22.5% were referred to children's social care,
- 17% had required a social work assessment,
- 14.3% had been a child in need, and
- 11.1% had been in need because of concerns about abuse or neglect.

Children under five years of age as a category within itself remains a high-risk group and there are many reasons why this is so. Published reports and research that considers the extent of abuse and neglect identified in young children draws our attention to the all-important messages and themes of which early years practitioners should be aware.

Recognising the common themes and emerging risks factors for young children helps to raise awareness for early years practitioners enabling them to respond appropriately should they be concerned about a child. We will explore these many themes throughout the book and more so in chapter four when we consider how we identify risk factors in the early years.

Risk factors for the under twos – headline themes

Child homicides are most perpetrated by the child's parent or stepparent.

In 2019 this related to 31% of all child homicides. The Office for National Statistics (ONS) reported that children under the age of one have the highest rate of homicide.

Parent vulnerability

Serious case reviews highlight the extent to which parent vulnerability impacts upon children's wellbeing and safety. Parents identified as those needing most support include several pertinent factors.

- Parents with mental health issues.
- Parental substance misuse.
- Young parents.
- Adults with learning difficulties.

- Parents who have experienced abuse themselves.
- Women who requested termination of their pregnancy whose procedure was not carried out (usually because of late requests).

Source: The National Society for the
Prevention of Cruelty to Children (NSPCC)

Children under one year

It won't be surprising to hear that within the under fives our most vulnerable have been identified as those children under the age of one year. Contributing factors to babies' vulnerabilities include their fragility, early stages of development and their complete and utter dependence upon others to meet their physical, social and emotional needs. Babies are less resilient when exposed to the effects of malnourishment or maltreatment. They cannot speak out to inform others about their experiences or seek help from those who might otherwise be able to intervene to keep them safe and well.

In 2018 the Children's Commissioner for England reported on the extent to which babies under one were known to local authorities' social care. The report, A Crying Shame, noted that '19,640 babies under a year old identified by local authorities as being "in need", largely due to risk factors in the family home'. Within this overall statistic, 12,286 of these babies were deemed as specifically at risk of abuse and neglect. Other contributing factors that determined children's vulnerability included themes such as 'family disfunction' and families in 'acute stress'.

It is worth noting that when referencing babies known to local authorities, these will be children who have been referred to social care and who have been subject to a child in need (CIN) assessment. Of course, not all babies at risk will be known to statutory services meaning that the full extent of children exposed to risks and harms cannot be determined by a recognised statistic or realistic figure.

The number of serious incidents, including deaths, for under ones continues to rise. Notifications of serious incidents given by local authorities in England to the Child Safeguarding Practice Review Panel increased by 27% during the first half of 2020–2021 in comparison to the numbers for the same period from the previous year. These worrying figures sadly align with concerning reports from Ofsted's Chief Inspector Amanda Spielman who in November 2020 reported there had been 'an alarming 20% rise in babies being killed or harmed' in the first lockdown period due to the COVID-19 pandemic. This rise in incidents represented both intentional injuries to babies and sudden, unexpected deaths in babies. Spielman believed that the reasons for this sharp increase was due to the 'toxic mix' of isolation, poverty and mental illness that caused incidents to occur between March and October 2020 when lockdown in the UK was at its peak.

Learning from serious case reviews

Serious case reviews, now referred to as *safeguarding practice reviews* in England, or similar processes provide insight about the contributing factors that lead to the death of a child or a serious incident where abuse or neglect is known.

Babies are disproportionately represented in safeguarding practice reviews.

We have established that children under the age of one year are most vulnerable. Case review statistics not only draw attention to the extent of serious cases where young children are the subject, but they also identify the risks. They highlight relevant factors that are often overlooked or missed by professionals that indicate a child is in danger. They scrutinise the actions and efforts undertaken by those working with the child and their family to determine if appropriate and timely interventions took place. They conclude on what is understood to have happened to the child and what could have been done differently to have avoided or prevented harm.

The National Society for the Prevention of Cruelty to Children (NSPCC) summarised risk factors identified in case reviews for the under twos and there are a several reoccurring themes.

Abusive relationships and domestic abuse

Parents do not always understand that an abusive relationship can be harmful to their young children, particularly babies. Some adults will not recognise that the relationship is abusive in the first instance, and they will often be oblivious to the dangers failing to understand that 'domestic abuse poses a significant risk to a baby's wellbeing' (NSPCC, 2017). Unfortunately, these deficits in parents' knowledge and understanding about domestic abuse are not the only concern identified. Reviews also inform us that many professionals working with young children do not always appreciate the subtleties of domestic abuse and the detrimental effects it has upon babies or young children.

Another important element raised through review processes is that often professionals working with whole families forget to consider the experiences of babies and the under twos. Support for parents and older children in families who can communicate their needs will often be taken into account through assessment and risk management whereas the needs of babies who are unable to communicate are frequently missed and unrepresented.

Sudden unexpected deaths in infancy (SUDI)

Identified risks for very young children are not always those that occur directly as a result of intentional abuse or neglect. Case reviews also capture themes of sudden and unexpected deaths in babies. It is sometimes difficult to determine the reasons as to why the sudden death of a baby has transpired. Research into such tragedies does however give some indication as to the nature and circumstances for each child and family, particularly those most vulnerable. This serves to identify risks and provide interventions that have the potential to prevent harm to other children.

Research and data indicate the nature and circumstances for children at risk of SUDI. Findings in a report published by The Child Safeguarding Practice Review Panel (2020) recognised a number of risk factors for babies already identified as being vulnerable. These being:

- Parents who were co-sleeping with babies.
- Parental alcohol and drug use.
- Parental mental ill health.
- Evidence of neglect.
- Domestic abuse.
- Overcrowding, poor housing.
- Parental criminal conviction.
- Parents who were care leavers.
- Young parents.

The review recognised that the 'predisposing risks were often combined with out of usual incidents or situational risks'. Sometimes this meant that babies were even more vulnerable due to changes in family circumstances or if they were exposed to unsafe sleep environments. A number of contributing factors that increased risks for babies included:

- Moving to different accommodation.
- Attending a family party.
- Children of a parent with a new partner.
- Being unwell or ill.
- Children of adults using drugs or alcohol especially on the night when a tragic incident occurs.

It is important to recognise that many of the interventions that offer preventative solutions to SUDI are centred on advice about safe sleep, the care of babies and young children in the home and the appropriate and safe use of car seats and sleeping babies.

TIME TO THINK

Think of the children in your setting. What vulnerabilities do you identify? Think about the ages of the children, their families and their unique circumstances.

TEAM TALK

How do you identify or communicate recognised risks to children in your setting? How do you ensure that those who are most vulnerable are supported?

The impact of the COVID-19 pandemic upon young children's safety and wellbeing

The full extent of abuse, neglect and adverse experiences that young children were exposed to because of the COVID-19 pandemic is now becoming clearer.

The most alarming consequences especially during lockdown periods impacted upon vulnerable children. A review into the death of Arthur Lambinjo-Hughes, a five-year-old boy who suffered prolonged abuse and was murdered by his step mother concludes many consequential failings attributed to circumstances exacerbated by the isolation of the pandemic.

Unseen children

Children including newly born babies were simply not seen by anyone other than their immediate parents. The lack of or limitation of professional support from schools and childcare settings, extended family or a wider community meant that isolated children became invisible to the world outside of their immediate home environment. For many children already recognised as vulnerable this was catastrophic. Many children identified as requiring lower-level interventions had needs put on hold or support was delayed due to the pandemic crisis. A significant drop in referrals to children's social care during the first and second lockdown periods in the UK was attributed to the fact that schools, which usually account for most referrals, were less aware of children's need for statutory assistance.

A reduction in community-based universal services

Services such as those delivered from children's centres, parent groups or drop-in clinics where health visitors could check children's development and advise parents on a variety of preventative, health related topics ceased. The rise of SUDI was explained as being because of less preventative advice offered by professionals to new or young parents. Home visits were limited, and many didn't take place at all. Necessary meetings moved to online and face-to-face contact in person became a virtual reality, which greatly compromised the ability to safeguard and protect children.

Deficits in single and multi-agency practice

Working in partnership with other professionals to meet holistic needs that optimises outcomes for children is a proven and effective strategy. Over time, the breakdown in integrated approaches that have promoted multi-agency working within the children's workforce has meant that during a time of crisis there were less opportunities to respond to the needs of young children and their parents. Changes made to services that once offered 'joined up' working approaches that worked in partnership with early years practitioners had weakened the efforts in providing vital support for families.

The impact of the COVID-19 pandemic upon the early childhood workforce

Working in the early years during a pandemic has been a momentous challenge. Just like other professionals working with children, the pressures are widely acknowledged.

Health visiting services

Changes to health visiting services in England have been recognised as negatively impacting upon children pre-pandemic. A report by the Institute of Health Visiting published in December 2020 recognised that because of these changes, the 'reach' of health visitors had diminished for babies and young children who were already deemed invisible to other agencies. The report, State of Health Visiting in England, scrutinised the impact of COVID-19 upon the lives of babies and young children. It concluded that the service was 'ill-prepared for the consequences of the pandemic following years of austerity and plummeting health visiting workforce numbers'. Health visitors concerned about unseen children during the pandemic believed that it had further led to 'widening inequalities and increased safeguarding risks and need for children under five'.

Children's social care

In September 2020 some five months after an initial lockdown in the UK, the Local Government Association reported that during the height of lockdown the number of referrals to children's services social care had fallen by almost a fifth. It was an inevitable outcome. Referrals began to decline as children became out of sight from those who would under normal circumstances be able to identify concerns, listen and respond to disclosures of abuse or neglect, and generally advocate for children and take action. A survey conducted by the British Association of Social Workers asked social workers about their experiences during and immediately after the pandemic. Out of all surveyed, 77.7% believed that their 'experience of working under lockdown restrictions had increased their concerns about the capacity to safeguard or protect adults and children'. Social workers from all four nations in the UK acknowledged that there was a significant increase in referrals to social care, which in turn impacted upon their increasing caseloads by the autumn of 2020, the period when lockdowns eased. This relevant landmark represented the time when schools and early years settings were once again becoming fully operational. It was clear that as soon as children were in direct contact with professionals working with them, the full extent to which children were identified as needing support and protection became evident and could be addressed.

Early years provision – including schools

The pandemic presented numerous challenges for the early years workforce in respect to being able to effectively safeguard and protect children. Initial lockdowns resulted in many settings closing their doors until it was deemed safe to re-open once again. A limited number of early years settings were able to provide care for vulnerable children in line with Government criteria. Government data capturing school and day care attendance during the first lockdown showed concerningly low numbers. Of these numbers, many children were identified as those most in need.

The complexities surrounding the different kinds of childcare provided by an early years' workforce created challenges for lots of reasons. Childminders working from family homes were unable to continue to deliver services to children in the first instance. Some who were shielding themselves or family members were unable to operate for some time. Many nannies or home-based childcare practitioners working from family homes were unable to do so due to the hazards of coronavirus and serious risk of infection. Even when some settings were able to reopen, parents' reluctance to send their children to school or day care also added to the challenges as they tried to reach out to vulnerable children. For some parents the pandemic provided the perfect excuse to disengage with professionals and hide behind the COVID-19 crisis often at the expense of children's welfare and safety.

Early years settings and schools maintained contact with parents through phone calls or by sending messages. However, the lack of physical contact or visible presence for many young children meant that they were placed at further risk with little or no monitoring or most importantly, recognition of any new or emerging concerns. Early years settings that had closed or partially closed also had to grapple with the restrictions placed upon them as a result of staff being furloughed therefore reducing or restricting their availability to make welfare calls to children who were absent from childcare.

When further national lockdown restrictions came into place and schools closed once more, early years provisions remained open. This meant that within the wider professional context there was significant and greater reliance upon the early years workforce to be the sector with most potential to engage with children and families. The prevailing impact of the pandemic upon young children remains. Discussions between Ofsted and early years practitioners (2022) highlighted developmental concerns for children returning to childcare or for some attending for the first time after the pandemic. In their report Ofsted noted areas that had directly and negatively impacted upon children's wellbeing, namely,

- children's communication and language development,
- children's personal, social and emotional development, and
- a delayed physical development in babies.

TIME TO REFLECT

How because of the pandemic might the shortfalls in children's development directly impact upon their wellbeing and safety? What can be done to address this?

SHOWCASE – KIDZRUS NURSERY GROUP

KidzRus are a group of five nurseries operating in Salford, Greater Manchester. Salford is a city noted for its disadvantage and is one of the most deprived authorities in England. During the pandemic the nursery group actively developed ways to reach out to families who were struggling with the basic economic demands of family life by opening their own family food bank that operated from their nursery premises.

What informed and led to the development of the service?

Initially a home visit made by one of the nursery managers to a lone parent with two children under the age of three triggered a response to develop a food bank service pre-pandemic. Having worked alongside a local food bank initially, the group realised there was a need to support parents of children in their own nurseries. Stock for the food bank was created by increasing nursery food orders and by taking regular donations from parents who were happy to contribute to help others.

Respectful and free from stigma

The nurseries created opportunities for parents to collect food from a separate entrance in the nursery to protect the privacy of families and to create a safe and confidential space for them. Weekly food parcels were discretely placed at the rear of the nurseries' head office for parents to help themselves.

Developing children's understanding of empathy and acts of kindness

Children in the nursery were very much involved in the process by helping to stock the shelves with food donations and organising the food parcels that were sent out to family homes. By actively engaging children in the process the nursery believed it gave them an understanding of personal responsibility helping them to recognise that other children's circumstances may not necessarily be the same as their own. It also enabled children to play a meaningful role in offering them opportunities to act in ways that helped others who were in need.

What parents had to say

'I have never been as grateful for a few bags of shopping. I couldn't help the tears at the door as I was so overwhelmed. My children are so excited to tuck into the cakes and biscuits myself and my children thank you from the bottom of our hearts for your kindness.'

'Today I woke up wondering what I was going to do for food for the next week until I get paid. I have a two and a four year, who are now in isolation, and as a single mother with very little help, the thought of next week has been dreadful. I had spent the morning searching the foodbanks in the area, most needing food vouchers or money to pay before getting a food parcel or collection. I messaged the nursery family foodbank explaining my situation and within a couple of hours they had delivered me enough food to last me and my kids for the week completely free of charge. I'm still in awe that there is still so much kindness in the world despite the pandemic we are facing. Thank you so much you have made mine and my children's lives so much easier this week, I am forever grateful to you all.'

Key strategies that promote child-centred safeguarding and child protection practices in the early years

Underpinning knowledge

Educating adults about how they can safeguard and protect children has to be one of the most important strategies that is available to us when working with children. It is fundamental to all child-centred approaches and systems. Whilst we will explore a whole range of strategies in subsequent chapters, there are some key components that provide early years practitioners with firm foundations upon which to build and strengthen their knowledge base.

Education and training

When I first began to work with vulnerable children my greatest concern was that I knew very little about child protection. I was under confident and worried that my lack of knowledge would cause me to fail and more so that this would be to the detriment of the children with whom I was working. Post qualification training played a key role in equipping me with the knowledge I needed to fulfil my role. Effective safeguarding and child protection training will provide practitioners with various requirements upon which they should seek further knowledge. The basics of our understanding should include the following.

- Understanding the need to be legally compliant and what this means in practice.
- Recognising the roles and responsibilities of the practitioner(s).
- Identifying the things that impact negatively or adversely upon children and the extent to which this has bearing upon their wellbeing and safety.
- Knowing when and how to take action to help or protect children.

It concerns me that sometimes early years providers seem to over complicate the process of accessing and keeping up to date with training worrying that they will miss the latest themes that are trending on social media. Whilst safeguarding and child protection as a bespoke theme has its complexities, it is also pretty straight forward to understand and engage with.

To make it as simple as possible I have categorised the components of safeguarding and child protection and what practitioners need to know and understand into five distinct areas. I will refer to these again in subsequent chapters.

1   *Understand our role and responsibilities* – recognising and fulfilling specific duties within our role.
2   *Identify* – how and what is recognised as risks or threats to children.
3   *Help* – safeguarding children with emerging or low-level concerns through early help or early intervention processes.

4   **Protect** – concerns and levels of need that distinguish the requirement to protect children.
5   **Report/Manage** – (manage, for those with designated safeguarding lead responsibilities) the elements that involve taking action to protect children and contributions to and engagement in processes that achieve this.

Regular investment in relevant and effective training empowers and equips practitioners with the appropriate knowledge, which ultimately demonstrates their commitment to meet the needs of children with whom they work.

Acquiring knowledge

Not all essential knowledge is acquired through formal training. Learning from experienced practitioners who provide good role models offering examples of practice that centre on the child is a powerful strategy. Recognising others who can help us to develop knowledge and skills is also important. This might be a work colleague such as a team leader or manager. It may be another professional working with you in support and a child or family. A health visitor or social worker. Taking time to learn from their experiences and perspectives can be helpful. We often learn more when we learn from each other. This collegial approach to acquiring knowledge from each another must however be reciprocated for it to be most effective. Be mindful that you may be the influencer in this working relationship and that others are looking to you for guidance. If you are a leader or a manager do not assume that team members know the same things that you know. Take account of your own journey and help someone else benefit from the things that you have learned. A skilled and competent leader will always find ways to provide inexperienced practitioners with the things they need to become efficient and effective in their own practice. We will look at leadership roles in more detail when we consider the role of the designated safeguarding lead in chapter three.

Active engagement

Without a doubt it will be the experiences and opportunities to engage with safeguarding and child protection processes that provide early years practitioners with meaningful lessons in how to develop their own practice. Reflecting upon my own journey, I recognise several key learning milestones from which I gained invaluable knowledge and experience of working with vulnerable children and families. These experiences were the basis upon which I was able to build effective practice and use it to inform an understanding of what might be happening for a child, giving me the confidence to make informed decisions and take necessary actions.

Being professionally curious

Professional curiosity is an important principle for everyone working with children and families. When we are *professionally curious*, we apply strategies that demonstrate effective safeguarding and child protection practice. When faced with a situation or circumstance that raises concerns about a child, we will do everything possible to determine fact, analyse a situation and assess risk. When practitioners are professionally curious, they will not take things at face value. They will combine several factors including looking, listening, asking direct questions, reflecting upon a situation and not making assumptions. This might involve seeking clarity about a situation from other professionals who may be working with the child or family. Case reviews often quote a lack of professional curiosity as a weakness, which unfortunately has tragic consequences for children.

Things that we should be particularly curious about:

- Significant adults in a child's life.
- Who the child lives with including extended family members, friends or those in relationships with the child's parents.
- Known risks to the child including specific vulnerabilities for the child and the parent/carers.
- Changes in circumstances that compromise or negatively impact upon a parent/carers ability to provide protective factors for a child.

It might be difficult or feel awkward to put ourselves in a position where we are asking questions about families and their personal circumstances. A child-centred approach to working with families always considers the risks for the child, the 'what ifs' and always puts the child's welfare first.

Understanding children's lived experiences

We cannot adopt a more child-centred approach than that of understanding and responding to children's lived experiences. Understanding children's day-to-day experiences helps us to put into perspective what life is like for them. Children living in a home where domestic abuse frequently occurs will experience multiple adverse consequences. For example, they may be persistently anxious, worried, and nervous about when the next incident or outburst will occur. They may experience intimidation, fear or blame having been told that is it their fault as to why the perpetrator behaves as they do towards their victim. Children often worry about a parent whom they want to protect but cannot. Seeing the situation from the child's experience means that we understand better the impact it has upon their wellbeing and safety. Whilst all abusive experiences for children should be acknowledged from their perspective, children who experience neglect particularly require practitioners to take their lived experiences into account. Neglect is often a long-drawn-out series of events for a child that has damaging consequences. A child that encounters neglect needs practitioners to consider what it is like for them to be constantly hungry, tired, ignored or rejected by unresponsive parents. They may also be rejected, isolated and ostracised by their peers because they are unclean and present as having poor hygiene. Being able to identify a child's lived experience should drive us to take prompt and appropriate actions to prevent abuse or neglect from continuing.

TIME TO THINK

Think of a child that you may have supported or who you are currently working with. How have the strategies identified in this chapter enabled you to work effectively with them and their families in identifying concerns for their wellbeing or safety and taking appropriate actions?

TEAM TALK

Discuss with your colleagues the extent by which your setting uses professional curiosity as a principle and approach that support effective safeguarding and child protection practices.

Part two: the wonder of the early years. Investment and focus on vulnerability past and present

I have experienced first-hand the numerous developments and changes in the early years especially in relation to supporting vulnerable children. There have been a number of significant developments over time many of which are no longer seen as specialist services, or their services have simply morphed into other types of early years provision delivered predominantly through the private, voluntary and independent sector.

• *Local authority, social services day care*

Historically it was local authority social service run day care that provided vulnerable children and families with specific and, in some instances, specialised support. The criteria for children who attend varied mostly focussed on children in need of protection. Many of the children were deemed 'child in need', some on child protection plans or cared for by the local authority. Whilst most children were those supported by social care this local authority funded provision also met a wider range of needs. These included:

- Children with disabilities or illness.
- Children in foster care or those living permanently with extended family members such as grandparents.
- Bereaved children experiencing the loss of a parent.
- Children of families fleeing domestic violence living in temporary accommodation such as homeless hostels.
- Children whose parents required respite because of personal or family crisis.
- Children with non- or poor speech and language.

Referrals to the service were taken predominantly from social workers or health visitors and places allocated to only those who met strict criteria.

I spent the formative years of my career working in social care day nurseries. On reflection they offered absolute lifelines to children and families. However, due to the service being targeted at the most disadvantaged children, the lack of wider integration with other children did little to combat stigma and the notion that this specialist childcare was for broken families only. High staffing and running costs led to most local authority nurseries offering childcare to paying customers alongside of those places earmarked for the neediest of children. Few of these nurseries remain in England and those that continue to operate do so within the same context of other universal childcare provision.

• *Children and family centres*

One of the earliest models of provision for young children that encompassed the wider needs of children were those services delivered from family centres. Many family centres opened in the early 1970s and continued to offer services until most merged into or became Sure Start Children's Centres in the late 1990s and early 2000s. The family centre model emerged as a response to the dissatisfaction that social care nurseries were limited in their ability to address the wider issues for children that involved working with parents. A 'switch from day care to family centres' provided opportunities for 'social work professionals to work with parents and children together'(Makins 1997).

Predominantly a local authority funded provision, family centre services were delivered by the public and voluntary sector.

Whilst family centres were a prerequisite to Sure Start Children's Centres, much of their work involved similar themes and principles. They often operated in areas of deprivation and their vision was very much directed at meeting the holistic needs of children and families. Coordination of wider services was a key feature, effectively delivered by a multi-agency team of professionals who worked together drawing upon each other's strengths and expertise.

In addition to offering early education for children, family centres provided other services such as:

*   Drop-in play sessions for parents and children.
*   Toy libraries.
*   Nurture groups for children in need.
*   Health groups and clinics.
*   Therapeutic groups for parents.
*   Parenting courses.
*   Training and employment opportunities.
*   Multi-professional hub for meetings and child protection conferences.

For many children, family centres proved a catalyst from where their safeguarding and child protection needs could be met. The nature of integrated working in this way enabled better identification of need, potential for swift early interventions to take place and the increased likelihood of effective information sharing and joint working with other professionals.

• *Sure Start Local Programmes and Children's Centres*

Sure Start Local Programmes (SSLPs) were initially established in 1999 under a new Labour Government. Funding of £450 million was committed to set up 250 SSLPs in 'areas with a very high concentration of children under four living in poverty' (Belsky et al. 2007). Each programme had a geographic catchment area that reached roughly 700 children. Its primary focus was to become the cornerstone in Labour's strategy addressing the detrimental impact of poverty upon young children. The programmes intentions were to 'integrate health, education and social welfare services'. By 2003 the Government had succeeded in their commitment to increase the number of what had now become Sure Start Children's Centres to 3,500, providing a centre for every community in England by 2010. Early intervention services were at the heart of Children's Centres. Whilst accessible to all families, the core features of the initiative were that those families who needed the most support should be targeted and reached with greater effort and vigour. Having personal experience of developing such services over a thirteen-year period, my own reflections are that the biggest jewel in the crown of Sure Start Children's Centres was the intentional drive to bring together multi-agency practitioners to work together to best meet children's needs. This often included co-location of staff across a number of disciplines and, most importantly, common and shared purposes delivered in partnership to children and families. The impact of this initiative was extraordinary, and the benefits provided children with life chances they otherwise would not have experienced or achieved. By 2011 the number of Sure Start Children's Centres peaked at 3,620. From herein with a change in Government, centres began to either close or merge. In June 2019 the Department for Education reported that out of the remaining 3,050 only 2,350 children centres existed. There were a further 700 children centre linked sites (DfE 2019).

• *Funded childcare and education for disadvantaged two-year-olds*

Driven by a wealth of evidence-based research into the long-term problems that disadvantaged children face because of poor and sometime adverse experiences in the first two years of their lives, funding for the disadvantaged two-year-olds initiative aims to help give children opportunities to catch up with their otherwise advantaged peers. The initiative, which has developed over several years, currently remains in place across England, Wales and Scotland and is delivered within the context of universal childcare provision.

Working with vulnerable children and families

It is fair to say that with the introduction of the two-year-old funded places for disadvantaged children came a wave of new experiences for the early years workforce as they were introduced to and indeed began to meet the needs of some very vulnerable young children. For many this involved them embracing a steep learning curve regarding understanding and experiencing the complexities of family lives for disadvantaged children. Contemporarily, this led to providers becoming engaged with numerous safeguarding incidents and occurrences in the lives of children they were working with. This gave countless challenges to early years practitioners. Over time and with less support for vulnerable children delivered predominantly through the public services, early years provision has mostly picked up the full tab of responsibility. As a result, the early years sector, including those working in education, are expected to take on increased safeguarding responsibilities for children.

TIME TO REFLECT

Think of your experience as a practitioner working with vulnerable children. Are you able to recognise challenges that have occurred because of changes over time? What do you think are the remaining challenges currently?

What makes the early years so unique?

I cannot emphasise enough the strengths that exist in the early years enabling practitioners to make informed responses that have the potential to safeguard and protect children. There are many things that make this possible and indeed unique to the sector.

Early years expertise is grounded in child development

Child development knowledge and expertise is central to being able to meet a child's holistic needs. Early years practitioners are experts when it comes to child development. Early years pedagogy, how we educate children and support their development, is central to meeting children's individual and distinctive needs. Knowledge of child development drawn upon by practitioners and used to inform effective safeguarding and child protection practice enables specific things to happen.

- It provides a baseline of expectations for age-appropriate child development. This helps practitioners to recognise when development is delayed, impaired and/or less than expected.
- Child development is used to inform accurate assessment of children that in turn determine appropriate support or interventions.
- Understanding how healthy development is achieved and recognising factors that prevent or impair a child's development is key to identifying concerns for them. Knowledge of neuroscience, the science behind brain development, also helps us to understand the significant impact of adverse experiences of abuse or neglect upon a child and/or what the effects of such experiences have upon their rapidly developing brain and nervous system. This prompts swift and appropriate responses that can be taken to intervene or act.

Early years practitioners foster trusting and enabling relationships with parents and carers

Early years practitioners are often perceived by parents as being non-threatening and supportive. This means that if in a situation where parents may be reluctant to engage with other agencies, early years practitioners are well positioned to influence and encourage parents to work with them. This makes for excellent partnership work, especially between the sector and statutory services. Working in partnership with parents offers multiple and ongoing opportunities to help them keep their children safe and well. Early years practitioners are well positioned to offer a wide range of support to parents such as:

- Advice and support about their child's development.
- Information about preventative safeguarding measures for children such as safe sleep initiatives or child safety advice.
- Signposting of information or facilitating introductions to other services that can provide expert help on specific needs for children and families.
- Guidance and support during difficult or stressful situations and acting as advocates helping them to navigate their way through multi-agency practice and engagement.

The invaluable role of the key person

The concept or idea of having a key person to work directly alongside of children and their parents is not a new to the early years. Almost 30 years ago we were advocating improved ways to support young children by developing a key person system that best met their social, emotional and physical needs when they attended childcare provision. The concept of enabling closer relationships with a child, their parents and the practitioner was explored through the work of Elinor Goldschmied and Sonia Jackson. Their publication 'People Under Three', published in 1994, led to lots of conversations and debate about the role of a child's key worker. Both professionals in their own right, Goldschmied and Jackson combined their expertise on the management of day care services, social work and child welfare to introduce a new and thought-provoking concept to early years practice. Integral to the development of the key person role they encouraged a number of fundamental practices for consideration. They recommended that key persons visit the child in the family home before they began attending nursery. That they help to settle the child and use 'intimate knowledge of their particular child' to aid relationships between the nursery and other 'specialists' working with the child such as 'speech therapists, health visitors, physiotherapists, social workers or community physicians'. They believed that the key person would be responsible for 'assessment, monitoring and record keeping'. This being particularly significant where a child had additional needs or had experienced abuse and neglect. Goldschmied and Jackson also recognised that apart from the child's parents, the key person was 'the one who knew most about a child with whom they spend so many hours of the day'.(Goldschmied and Jackson 1994).

Many of the early principles of the key person are reflected in the practices underpinned by the Early Years Foundation Stage statutory framework (2021).

This role, unique to the early years offers vast opportunities that identify children's needs, which can subsequently provide them with help and protection.

- Key persons have opportunities to gain an understanding of children's experiences both at home and in the setting.
- They develop relationships with parents or carers helping them to build a picture of what a child's 'lived experience' is like.
- Key persons can recognise any changes in a child's behaviour that might raise concerns. They easily identify other causes for concern such as a deterioration in a child's wellbeing.
- A child may choose to disclose abuse or neglect to their key person given the nature of their unique relationship.
- Practitioners who are key persons have opportunities to see the child most frequently and consistently unlike other professionals who might be working with the child.
- Key persons are best placed to monitor progress towards achieving agreed outcomes set out in plans such as those featured in early help, child in need or child protection processes.

EARLY YEARS SHOWCASE – PORTICO NURSERY GROUP

Portico nursery group managers shared their experiences of how they use the role of the key person to aid and support vulnerable children in their nurseries.

Trusting relationships that help to recognise changes in children's behaviours

Managers in the nurseries acknowledge the role of the key person as being 'so important in recognising changes in children's behaviours by practitioners who know their children well'. The role enables children and parents to feel safe and comfortable with practitioners as they develop relationships that are built upon trust. This means that their position as key persons help them to address any concerns they may have for children.

The role as a catalyst for joint working

Whilst it might be the key person who initially raises concerns the team work together to discuss, assess and monitor a situation. The designated safeguarding leads and SENDCO conduct regular checks with key persons and have meetings with staff where concerns can be discussed.

One child who began attending nursery had never interacted with other children or adults. From the very first session during the 'settling in period' the key person recognised some concerns which they were able to share with the child's parent. The nursery was quick to respond to the identified needs of the child resulting in them accessing help and advice for the child's parent.

Early years – a marginalised sector

Having considered the unique position and opportunities that early years practitioners hold in recognising and responding to the safeguarding needs of young children the sector should be confident both in respect to its role and status.

Practitioners should be confident in their knowledge, experience and position in engaging with a whole range of processes that form part of a resolve for children. Unfortunately, my own experiences and those of others would suggest that this is not always the case. In reality the truth is that if you are an early years practitioner you will often find yourself fighting your corner, raising your hand to be recognised and standing your ground on a matter of knowing more about the child with whom you work with on a regular basis.

The sector remains frequently marginalised, misunderstood and de-valued often by other professionals and as a result, sadly by itself. When this happens, it can lead to doubt in our own abilities and relevance which in turn influences our capacity to act effectively for the children we care for. I get disheartened when I hear about experiences from people working in early years especially when working within multi-agency safeguarding partnerships. There is still a shortfall and lack of recognition of all that the sector does and can do to support children. It is fair to say that not all view the sector negatively, but I sense that a substantial shift is still needed to address the issues created through ignorance and assumptions by others that early years practitioners are just not up to the job.

Recently whilst delivering designated safeguarding lead training I was explaining the process of challenge and escalation within social care. A concerned childminder asked 'What if someone more professional than me tells me I'm wrong'? The process of escalation usually occurs when there is disagreement between two agencies about an outcome for a child. I was explaining that early years practitioners, including childminders, would be able to challenge other agencies or another person's perspective and decision making if they considered it to be wrong. The childminder felt insecure and uncertain as to how she would do this and was intimidated by what she perceived as coming from a place of deficit. In her mind even though she was extremely experienced both in years and knowledge she believed that others would be better able to make decisions and judgements about a situation because of their perceived more important, relevant role and status as a professional. In her mind she had excluded herself from the process. We still have much more to do to impart confidence to a sector that does not always consider itself worthy of representation. This in part might be due to the lack of self-belief instilled in us by others because of negative past experiences. Or as with the concerned childminder, it might be that we worry that we are not enough and there is always someone else who can do a better job at safeguarding and protecting children than we can.

TIME TO REFLECT

Have you ever been made to feel that your contributions to processes that safeguard or protect a child were less than valuable in comparison to those offered by other professionals? How do you now view this in light of our considerations of the unique position that working in the early years offers?

Key messages from chapter one

- Young children especially those under the age of five are a highly vulnerable group and their vulnerabilities are prevailing.
- Risks for children in the early years continue to increase.
- Child-centred practices delivered by an early years' workforce has greater potential to safeguard and protect children.
- A declining and dedicated investment in early years provision has resulted over time in the current sector taking full or greater responsibility for the most vulnerable of children.
- Early years practitioners provide children with unique opportunities that safeguard and protect them.
- Practitioners working in the early years sector are often marginalised and not always recognised for their valuable contributions towards safeguarding processes and procedures.

References

Belsky, J., Barnes, J., and Melhuish, E. (2007). *The National Evaluation of Sure Start. Does Area-based Intervention Work?* Bristol: Policy Press.

Bilson, A., and Martin, E.C. (2017). Referrals and Child Protection in England: One in Five Children Referred to Children's Services and One in Nineteen Investigated before the Age of Five. *The British Journal of Social Work*, Volume 47, Issue 3, Pages 793–811.

The Child Safeguarding Practice Review Panel. (2020). *Out of Routine: A Review of Sudden Unexpected Death in Infancy in Families Where the Children Are Considered at Risk of Significant Harm*. Crown copyright 2020. Final Report.

Community Care. (2020). *'Covid Pressure Cooker' Behind 20% Rise in Reports of Serious Harm to Babies, Says Inspectorate Head*. Ofsted speech by Amanda Spielman.

A Crying Shame. (2018, October). *Office of the Children's Commissioner*. Children's Commissioner for England.

Department for Education. (2019). *Numbers of Children's Centres, 2003 to 2019: Annual Figures for the Number of Children's Centres from 2003 to 2019 Ad-hoc Notice*. Department for Education.

Goldschmied, E., and Jackson, S. (1994). *People Under Three*. Routledge.

Gov.UK. (2022). *Education Recovery in Early Years Providers: Spring 2022*. Gov.uk.

Local Government Association (LGA). (2020, September). *Children's Social Care Referrals Fell by a Fifth During Lockdown* (www.local.gov.uk)

Makins, V. (1997). *Not Just a Nursery. Multi-agency Early Years Centres in Action*. London: National Children's Bureau.

NSPCC. (2017). Summary of risk factors and learning for improved practice around working with children aged two and under. *Infants: Learning from Case Reviews*.

Serious Notification Incidents – Part 1 (April to September) 2020–21. GOV.UK. Explore Education Statistics (explore-education-statistics. service.gov.uk).

Social Work During the Pandemic – The British Association of Social Work (BSWA). (2021, January). *The Professional Association for Social Work and Social Workers* (basw_social_working_during_the_covid_19_pandemic_ initial_findings_26.01.21.pdf)

State of Health Visiting in England. (2020, December). *Institute of Health, Visiting Excellence in Practice* (State-of-Health-Visiting-survey-2020-FINAL-VERSION-18.12.20.pdf)

Recognising and responding to abuse and neglect in early childhood

In this chapter we will consider definitions of abuse and neglect and how this presents in young children. In chapter one and in reference to the components mentioned that early years practitioners need to know when engaging with safeguarding and child protection processes, chapter two is centred on the need to *identify*.

Identify – captures the features required in order to recognise children's needs both initially and over time. It acknowledges risk and considers unique circumstances for each child. It considers the child's lived experiences which on turn facilitate decisions that enable appropriate responses to take place.

What is abuse?

Abuse is a form of maltreatment of a child. Somebody may abuse or neglect a child by inflicting harm, or by failing to act to prevent harm. Harm can include ill treatment that is not physical as well as the impact of witnessing ill treatment of others. This can be particularly relevant, for example, in relation to the impact on children of all forms of domestic abuse. Children may be abused in a family or in an institutional or community setting by those known to them or, more rarely, by others. Abuse can take place

DOI: 10.4324/9781003137054-2

wholly online, or technology may be used to facilitate offline abuse. Children may be abused by an adult or adults, or another child or children.

HM Gov (2018)

Categories of abuse and neglect

Whilst there are various types of child abuse, I want to explore the four categories which are, neglect, emotional, physical, and sexual abuse. Definitions may vary slightly depending upon different guidance available in the UK. I have chosen to reference 'What to do if you are worried a child is being abused'. Advice for practitioners (HM Gov 2015) to describe the four categories. Having the ability to use and apply such definitions described in Government guidance provides opportunities to not only understand what each category means but most importantly to inform other important processes. Referencing or using these categories will help to achieve the following.

- Recognise abuse and neglect within the context of harm to a child.
- Clarify the situation from the child's perspective.
- Support decision making and determine actions needed to be taken to safeguard or protect a child.

All practitioners working with children should know and understand the definitions. Designated safeguarding leads, those making professional judgements and taking actions to help and protect children will use knowledge and application of definitions to support their role and to fulfil their safeguarding responsibilities.

Neglect

Neglect is a pattern of failing to provide for a child's basic needs, whether it be adequate food, clothing, hygiene, supervision, or shelter. It is likely to result in the serious impairment of a child's health or development.

Children who are neglected often also suffer from other types of abuse. It is important that practitioners remain alert and do not miss opportunities to take timely action. However, while you may be concerned about a child, neglect is not always straightforward to identify.

Neglect may occur if a parent becomes physically or mentally unable to care for a child. A parent may also have an addiction to alcohol or drugs, which could impair their ability to keep a child safe or result in them prioritising buying drugs, or alcohol, over food, clothing, or warmth for the child.

Neglect may occur during pregnancy as a result of maternal drug or alcohol abuse.

Recognising neglect in young children

- A child's basic needs are not met due to inadequate food, clothing, warmth, hygiene, and/or medical care including oral health.
- Deterioration in the child's wellbeing including weight loss and poor presentation.
- Poor or no attachment with significant adults.
- Failure to thrive – development milestones are delayed such as speech and language development or significant delays in physical development. Scottish Government guidance refers to *'faltering growth'* which is an 'inability to reach normal weight and growth or development milestones in the absence of medically discernible physical and genetical reasons' (2021).
- Poor supervision of a child, such as being left in the care of another child or unsuitable adult.
- A child abandoned or left alone.

Prolonged neglect

Responding to neglect can be rather challenging particularly in relation to lower levels of neglect, given that it often requires a pattern of incidences or repeated occurrences that take time to determine or recognise that a child is indeed experiencing neglect.

Addressing serious neglect

Neglect (and abuse) can occur over time and be an accumulation of events or situations. It can also represent as a one-off incident that happens placing a child at risk of health impairment, developmental delay or significant harm.

Whilst neglect over time is seriously harmful, single instances of neglect can literally be life threatening.

- A child left unsupervised or poorly supervised is considered as neglectful on the part of the responsible parent or adult.
- A child who does not receive appropriate medical attention whether as a preventive measure or due to injury or illness is experiencing neglect.

Taking timely action

As a manager, I remember a three-year-old child returning to nursery after the weekend with an injury to the top of her foot. The area of the injury was raised, it was very red and swollen. The injury had not been there on the Friday we had last seen them, and it was now Monday. This child was on a child protection plan due to neglect and her mom with whom she lived could not explain the injury, which had become clearly infected. In addition to this she had not attempted to seek medical attention for her daughter over the weekend. When the child was taken to hospital by the family's social worker the child was immediately admitted as she had developed Sepsis. Doctors confirmed the seriousness of the infection and noted that prompt action taken had literally saved her life. Attendance at nursery for this little girl and the actions taken by vigilant staff resulted in her being protected. It could have been a very different outcome indeed.

Zara's story

There was a much bigger story for the child mentioned previously and her family. Mom, Zara (not her real name), had three children aged eleven, three and one. The nursery which was part of a Sure Start Local Programme cared for Zara's two youngest children and as a single parent she received help from the family support workers in the wider Sure Start team. Her eldest child at eleven years was attending school. The main concerns for Zara were her dependency upon alcohol and drugs and the fragile state of her mental health. This made it difficult for her to meet the needs of her three children all of whom she loved dearly. Her inability to address her own personal addictions had catastrophic consequences upon her children. Until she was able to address her own needs, her capacity to meet those of her children's was seriously compromised. Because of the incident with the untreated injury and on the day that her daughter was admitted to hospital all three children were removed from Zara and placed into foster care. Sometimes child neglect can occur because of the inability of parents, for whatever reason, to offer children safety and protection. We will return to Zara's story in chapter six.

The links between poverty, disadvantage and neglect

Not all neglect is as a result of adverse experiences in the lives of adults, and it is not always due to poor economic status or disadvantage. We do however know that neglect and indeed child abuse are often linked to poverty and the impact that poverty has upon children's lives both in the short and long term. The association between poverty and child abuse and neglect in the UK is a much-debated topic.

The Joseph Rowntree Foundation, an independent social change organisation, is known for its research and work done to address poverty in the UK. In 2016 it produced a report drawing upon an evidence review it had undertaken into the relationship between poverty, child abuse and neglect. The report considered two key aspects. First, how poverty affected a child's chance of being abused or neglected and second, the impact abuse or neglect in childhood has on poverty in adult life. Whilst the report recognised that variances in data collection in the UK made it difficult to state a clear and simple conclusion, it did determine that there is a 'strong association between families' socio-economic circumstances and the chances that their children will experience child abuse and neglect'. Bywaters et al. (2016) recognised risk factors that were both direct and indirect impacts of poverty.

- Parenting capacity, for example affected by mental and/or physical illness or learning disabilities.

- Capacity to buy or provide better environment conditions.
- External neighbourhood factors: the social and physical environment.
- Negative adult behaviours, for example domestic violence or substance use, perhaps provoked or exacerbated by family stress.

In 2021 and at the peak of a global pandemic, the Joseph Rowntree Foundation further reported that the impact of coronavirus would lead to more significant impact upon families for both those experiencing poverty and the 'working poor', those working but whose income is significantly low. The full impact of COVID-19 prevails, however what is clear is that the economic impact has put pressures on groups who were already at higher risk of poverty – for example, those working in low paid sectors, minority ethnic groups and lone parents (Joseph Rowntree Foundation 2021).

Neglect in affluent families (affluent neglect)

Neglect can also occur to children who are from affluent families and where their materialistic needs are met more than adequately. This however does not mean that they won't experience neglect. Affluent neglect is often overlooked or dismissed because the notion of affluence and neglect may appear to be contradictory. It can also be obscured due to children's care being met by those employed to do so such as nannies or home-based child carers. Children from affluent families may experience neglect similarly to other children in a number of ways.

- Poor/non-supervision.
- Medical needs not being met.
- Educational needs not met.

It is also particularly difficult to recognise especially as it often manifests through emotional neglect, which can be hard to identify.

Bernard (2018) explored how social workers engaged with neglectful parents from affluent backgrounds. It identified some unique elements about affluent neglect.

- The ideas of neglect in families who are affluent may not be considered or they are dismissed.

- Child neglect may be under reported in affluent communities.
- Parents will often have the financial resources to engage with legal processes to deter or prevent actions being taken against them by statutory services.

Strategies that identify and respond to neglect

- Understanding child development including neuroscience, the development of the brain.

Drawing upon our knowledge and expertise of child development in the early years provides opportunities to recognise the negative impact upon a child's otherwise healthy development as a result of neglect. This includes knowledge of what is needed for healthy brain development in young children and the effects of adverse experiences upon brain development in a child's formative years.

- Understanding and seeing things from the child's lived experience.

Having regular and frequent contact with a child who is experiencing neglect provides early years practitioners with possibilities that identify and respond to children's experiences as they are happening and unfolding.

- Communicating the impact of neglect upon the child with others.

Once more, regular contact with early years practitioners and children offers a credible and relevant account of how neglect impacts upon their behaviours and wellbeing. This provides important information to others who may not know the child very well or see them often.

- Use of chronological record keeping and reporting.

Recording over time and in a chronological order, the order of what happened and when, helps to build a picture of what is happening for a child. An important and vital aspect to any recording process, chronological accounts help to build a picture over time especially where neglect is a concerned. This helps with decision making to inform when it is necessary to take action and/or seek support from others.

- Recognising when appropriate interventions are required.

Understanding the levels of need for a child is the responsibility of every practitioner working with children in the early years and not that of the designated safeguarding leads alone. Knowing when to act, for example at a lower level of concern that can be addressed through early interventions or early help processes, can prevent the needs of a child from escalating and getting worse.

- Engaging others to take action.

If the needs of a child demonstrate that the extent of neglect is significantly harmful for and dangerous for a child, statutory service such as the police or social care will need to be informed.

TIME TO THINK

Think of a child that you may have identified as experiencing neglect.

- What were the signs that gave you reasons to believe the child was neglected?
- What actions did you take? If your concerns were shared with other professionals, what was their response?
- Given that neglect can sometimes be difficult to identify, how long did it take before any appropriate actions were taken to support the child?

Emotional abuse

Emotional abuse is the persistent emotional maltreatment of a child. It is also sometimes called psychological abuse and it can have severe and persistent adverse effects on a child's emotional development.

Although the effects of emotional abuse might take a long time to be recognisable, practitioners will be in a position to observe it, for example, in the way that a parent interacts with their child. Emotional abuse may involve deliberately telling a child that they are worthless, or unloved and inadequate. It may include not giving a child opportunity to express their views, deliberately silencing them or 'making fun' of what they say or how they communicate.

Emotional abuse may involve serious bullying – including online bullying through social networks, online games or mobile phones – by a child's peers.

Recognising emotional abuse in young children

- Developmental delay.
- Significant language delay or poor speech and language.
- Poor or no attachment between the child and their parents/carers.
- A child who is anxious and afraid.
- Children who appear fearful in the presence of certain adults or older siblings, family friends or relatives.
- A child with low self-esteem.
- A child who is aggressive or cruel towards other children or animals.

A child experiencing emotional abuse who is already known to a practitioner may be identified as such because;

- their behaviour has significantly changed,
- they become withdrawn or set themselves apart from others, or
- they become aggressive or display challenging behaviours such as bullying or being unkind to others.

A child who regresses in their behaviour or who momentarily has setbacks in their development such as regular or frequent toileting accidents may do so because they are being emotionally harmed.

Emotional abuse can often occur if a child experiencing a traumatic event in the home. We know that if children hear or see domestic abuse or violence it is extremely damaging to their emotional wellbeing. Domestic abuse can also include behaviours that are controlling or coercive. A child may have learned how to comply with such manipulative behaviours to achieve calm and reduce tension. They may be scapegoated by adults or falsely blamed for being the reason as to why an angry or aggressive adult or young person behaves as they do. These experiences for children signify emotional abuse. We should not however assume that all abuse happens in the home. There has been an increase in the amount of child-to-child abuse particularly in schools and as a result of children engaging with others online. We will look at both topics in greater detail in chapter four. It is evident that out of all the categories emotional abuse can be the most difficult to recognise. Unlike other types of abuse where symptoms and indicators are more visible or noticeable, it is harder to determine the outward symptoms of emotional abuse.

Emotional abuse is also associated with other categories of abuse. Let us be mindful that there are elements of emotional abuse in all abusive experiences for children and that it accompanies other categories of abuse including neglect.

We should be mindful that a child may disclose to a trusted adult or to someone who befriends them that they are being abused. Providing safe and nurturing environments for children will offer opportunities for them to speak out about their experiences with adults who care for them.

Liam's story

Liam was a three-year-old boy who along with his younger brothers and older sister attended the social services nursery I worked at in the early nineties. I was Liam's key worker and he and his sister will always come to mind especially when I think about the impact of child abuse upon young children. Frankly, this was one of the most awful examples of ongoing and persistent abuse of young children I had come across as an early year's practitioner. Liam and his brothers and sister were all on what was then referred to as the 'child protection register', now known as a child protection plan, because of neglect and emotional abuse. Liam's parents were young, his mom had given birth to Liam's sister as a teenager, dad was violent and both parents drank large amounts of alcohol. During the time that I worked with Liam, his mom gave birth twice and both babies were immediately removed from the parent's care. So much was going on for this family and the children were subjected to the most awful abuse. I distinctly remember times when Liam came into nursery crying and upset and us finding out this was because there had been an incident involving the police in the family home the night previously result-ing in Liam's dad being arrested and placed into police custody. One day we invited a police officer into the nursery as part of our 'people who help us' themed activity. On seeing the officer Liam ran screaming into another room to hide away. I also remember finding out that this vulnerable three-year-old was subjected to humiliating and degrading forms of punishment by his dad who would regularly make him wear a dress and mock him as punishment for his perceived wrongdoing. During the time that Liam attended the nursery I trained as a play therapist and used to offer therapy sessions for him knowing that he would benefit from the experience. The sessions mainly comprised initially of Liam aggressively throwing art materials around the room and him climbing on the windowsills. He did eventually begin to calm down and enjoy his sessions but there was a lot of therapeutic work to be done with Liam given the extent of his abuse. Liam and his brothers and sister were eventually removed from their parents and placed into foster care. All five children were adopted by an amazing family who agreed to keep the children together. I often wonder about them and hope that they recovered sufficiently to lead happy and fulfilling lives.

Strategies to identify and respond to emotional abuse

- Creating nurturing environments that are inclusive, representative of cul-ture, gender, race and children's individual identity.

When children are cared for within an environment that considers their unique and individual needs, they feel safe and secure.

- Providing language rich environments and opportunities to use language to express feelings.

Language development and communication play an important role when sup-porting children who experience abuse or neglect. If children experience emo-tional abuse and can communicate their feelings, practitioners can use these opportunities to take appropriate actions to safeguard and protect them. This can be done in groups or individually with children. One nursery reported that after introducing emotion cards as part of a small group activity to help children talk about feelings, they were able to support those who were experiencing parental conflict at home.

• Utilise the role of the key worker or named person to build effective and trusting relationships with children.

Each professional working with children will build relationships with them, enabling them to know and understand children's unique needs and personalities. This means that changes in a child's behaviour will be quickly identified and acted upon. Good relationships between parents and the key worker will also support a wider understanding of what a child's experiences are within the context of their own and wider family.

• Be prepared and able to respond to a child's disclosure.

Knowledge of how to respond to a child's disclosure of abuse or neglect is an important safeguarding feature for every early year's practitioner. Our role when working with children will require us to be skilled and capable practitioners who react and respond appropriately if a child tells them something that suggests they have experienced or if they are at risk of abuse or neglect. We will look at disclosure in more detail in chapter four.

TIME TO REFLECT

What might the psychological impact be upon a child's emotional health if they are afraid or anxious?

If a child is experiencing bullying at home how might this make them feel?

Physical abuse

Physical abuse is deliberately physically hurting a child. It might take a variety of different forms, including hitting, pinching, shaking, throwing, poisoning, burning, or scalding, drowning or suffocating a child.

Physical abuse can happen in any family, but children may be more at risk if their parents have problems with drugs, alcohol and mental health or if they live in a home where domestic abuse happens.

Babies and disabled children also have a higher risk of suffering physical abuse.

Physical harm may also be caused when a parent or carer fabricates the symptoms of, or deliberately induces, illness in a child. Physical abuse can also occur outside of the family environment.

Recognising physical abuse in young children

- Bruising, open wounds or injuries.
- Bruised or pinched areas such as ears.
- Bruising around the mouth, particularly in small babies indicating forced feeding.
- Hand marks/imprints of hand.
- Bruising on the arms, buttocks and thighs.
- Bite marks.
- Burns from cigarettes.
- Burns, marks from objects used to cause the burn. Blistered areas suggesting scalding such as immersing a child in hot bath water.
- Any bruising to a non-mobile baby, toddler or a child who is disabled or ill and therefore immobile should be viewed as suspicious.
- Broken blood vessels in the eyes suggesting shaking or trauma to the head, particularly in babies.
- A baby who appears unresponsive due to head trauma or injury.

There may be reasonable explanations as to why children become injured or physically harmed. However, there will be times when practitioners may become more concerned about a parent's response to their child's injury. For example:

- Their explanation for an injury is inconsistent with the injury.
- They change their minds about the reason for the injury.
- They cannot explain frequent or repeated minor injuries to a child.
- They have delayed seeking treatment for the injury.
- They have used different doctors or hospitals to treat the injury.

Smacking

The debate about smacking has been going on for years. The Oxford English Dictionary describes smacking at 'a sharp blow given with the palm of the hand' referring to it also being in a 'sudden and a violent way'. If we further cross reference this to the definition of physical abuse in this section, then really our conclusion should be that smacking is indeed a form of physical abuse given the references to 'hitting a child'. Smacking has for a long time been a rather grey area in terms of it being considered an acceptable form of 'reasonable punishment' by an adult towards a child. Without getting into the finer details and legality as reflected in current law, I believe that we cannot address physical abuse in children without at least acknowledging the subject of corporal punishment that presents as smacking.

The law and smacking

Scotland

The Scottish Government was the first in the UK to make smacking illegal. The Children (Equal Protection from Assault) (Scotland) Act 2019 was amended by removing the 'reasonable chastisement' defence from the Act making smacking illegal from 7 November 2020. From this date onwards all physical punishment or physical discipline is against the law. Scottish Government have taken into account that children have the same legal protection against assault as adults.

Wales

As a result of the passing of Children (Abolition of Defence or Reasonable Punishment) Act 2020 by the Welsh Assembly, as of 21 March 2022 physical punishment of children including smacking is illegal in Wales.

Laws in England and Northern Ireland currently do not legislate against smacking children. Government ministers in England have clarified that they intend not to legislate on the matter believing that by doing so would create a 'nanny state' that takes away the rights of parents who choose to use smacking as a means of punishment for their children.

The effects of smacking upon children.

- Smacking physically hurts and harms children.
- Smacking is emotionally damaging to a child, it makes them feel powerless, helpless and unable to defend or protect themselves.
- It makes them feel betrayed and ostracised.
- It demonstrates a lack of respect towards them and exhibits an imbalance of power between the adult and the child. Imbalance of power is a key feature in child abuse.
- Smacking gives children the impression that it's ok to use physical force towards or against another person.

TIME TO THINK

If you work in a country that legislates against smacking, how has this impacted upon your safeguarding and child protection practices?

How do you communicate with or respond to a parent who believes that it is acceptable to smack their child?

Strategies to identify and respond to physical abuse

- Practitioners are aware of what represents as a suspicious injury.

When working with young children it is important to acknowledge the differences between inevitable accidental injury that a child may sustain and those that occur because of non-accidental injury. Effective safeguarding training that enables practitioners to identify potential abuse is therefore vital for all who are working with children.

- Accurate and consistent recording of a child's injuries that occur both in the setting and outside of the setting should be undertaken by the practitioner.

Records of injuries should enable practitioners to recognise a number of things.

- What is the injury?
- Where on the child is the injury noted?

- What, if known, has happened to the child leading to them sustaining the injury?
- What actions were taken by the practitioner if the injury occurred whilst they were in their care?
- How was the injury communicated with parents/carers?

If the injury happened whilst the child was at home, somewhere other than the early years setting or in the case of nannies when the child was not being supervised by the practitioner, other factors should be considered.

- Who was the child with when the injury occurred?
- What happened that led to the child being injured?
- Does the explanation from the parent/carer about the injury and how the child obtained it seem feasible?
- Are there suspicious circumstances surrounding the child's injury?
- Is there a pattern or frequency occurring that requires further analysis and actions taken?
- All injuries that occur in non-mobile children should be considered suspicious and policies and practices regarding non-mobile injury protocols should be followed and adhered to.
- Birthmarks should be identified as such by medical professionals and recorded for further reference in the child's personal details.

Mongolian blue spot, which is a type of birthmark, is sometimes mistaken as being bruising on a baby. This category of birthmark can be present at birth or develop soon after birth. Mongolian blue spot is particularly common in children of African, Middle Eastern, Mediterranean or Asian heritage. All birthmarks should be noted to prevent a misdiagnosis of bruising or injury.

Bruising protocol for immobile babies and children exemplar

The bruising protocol for immobile babies and children, which forms part of the Greater Manchester Safeguarding Procedures strategy to protect babies and other immobile vulnerable children is an excellent example of a child-centred strategy underpinned by an uncompromising and explicit objective to protect children.

Protocol for injuries in non-mobile children, adapted from Wigan Safeguarding Partnership's injuries protocol flowchart.

Professional observes signs of possible injury in a child who is not independently mobile.

YOU MUST FOLLOW THE LOCAL SAFEGUARDING PARTNERS PROTOCOL

Arrange appropriate medical assessment and treatment in addition to following safeguarding procedures

If the child is seriously ill and requires emergency treatment call 999 and request an ambulance and the police

Seek an explanation, examine/observe injury and record accurately. This should include details of social history including other children and carers.

If you are a Health Professional observing what you think may be a birth mark:

See Health Professional Management of suspected Birth Mark

Explain to parents/carers that signs of possible injury in a child who is not independently mobile requires professionals to follow the Local Authority's Safeguarding Partners Protocol

A referral MUST be made immediately to a Paediatrician and Children's Social Care
1. Paediatrician on call for Child Protection Tel No ***** Out of hours ****

2. Children's Social Care Tel No **** Out of hours ****

3. Inform child's GP and Health Visitor / School Nurse

Signs and symptoms of possibly injury	
Bruises	Head injuries or signs of head injury
Abrasions and lacerations	Bleeding from the nose or mouth (could
Burns and scalds	indicate possible attempted suffocation)
Injury to the eye	Unexplained loss of consciousness or fits
	Pain, tenderness or failing to use an arm or leg

Figure 2.1 Protocol for injuries in non-mobile children, adapted from Wigan Safeguarding Partnership's injuries protocol flowchart.

The rationale for the protocol is to identify instances of when non-mobile children, predominantly babies under six months of age, sustain injuries that may have occurred because of child maltreatment.

It aims to protect those children who are not independently mobile. This includes babies 'not yet crawling, bottom shuffling, pulling to stand, cruising or walking independently'. It also refers to older children whose immobility is due to disability and children who have a loss of mobility either permanently or temporarily whether this loss of mobility is 'complete or partial'. This protocol is expected to be followed by all professionals working with children across a multi-disciplinary context. Working on the basis that bruising in non-mobile children is rare the response should always result in immediate consultation with children's services social care. On observing a sign of a possible injury in a child who is non-independently mobile, the observer should follow strict safeguarding procedures. As with any policy or procedure, an explanation of the rationale and expectations of what will happen should the protocol need to be followed should always be shared with parents. Not only does this provide clarity but helps parents to appreciate that its intentions are ultimately to safe-guard and protect their child. The rigorous approach to responding to injuries in non-mobile children is completely centred on the child, providing scrutiny and an immediate action response should a child need protection.

Example of a non-mobile injury protocol flowchart, adapted from one used by a Greater Manchester Local Authority.

An example of a flowchart that is expected to be followed when observing injuries in non-mobile children.

TIME TO REFLECT

Does your setting have a policy that specifically addresses concerns for children who are injured and are non-mobile? If so, how is this implemented? How do you communicate this with parents?

Sexual abuse

Sexual abuse is any sexual activity with a child. You should be aware that many children and young people who are victims of sexual abuse do not recognise themselves as such. A child may not understand what is happening and may not even understand that it is wrong. Sexual abuse can have a long-term impact on mental health. Sexual abuse may involve physical contact, including assault by penetration (for example, rape or oral sex) or non-penetrative acts such as masturbation, kissing, rubbing and touching outside clothing. It may include non-contact activities, such as involving children in the production of sexual images, forcing children to look at sexual images or watch sexual activities, encouraging children to behave in sexually inappropriate ways or grooming a child in preparation for abuse (including via the internet). Sexual abuse is not solely perpetrated by adult males. Women can commit acts of sexual abuse, as can other children.

Recognising sexual abuse in young children

- Children who are a withdrawn or fearful.
- Children who display inappropriate, sexualised behaviours towards other children and adults.
- Engaging in sexualised play, particularly role play with toys and/or other children.
- The use of sexual language that is applied in context.
- Physical symptoms such as injuries to the genitalia or anal areas. Bruising to buttocks, abdomens and thighs.
- Pain or itching of the genital areas.
- Sexually transmitted disease.
- Urinary infections.
- Continual and inappropriate or excessive masturbation.
- Children who show anxiety or unwillingness to remove clothes (for intimate care or changing reasons).
- Self-harm which may include eating disorders, especially in older children.

Strategies to identify and respond to sexual abuse

- Knowledge of the child that is built upon strong attachments and relationship between the child and their key person.

As previously stated, we cannot underestimate the importance of building secure and trusting relationships with children in order to identify the things that may compromise or threaten their wellbeing and safety. Practitioners will recognise that effective and supportive relationships with children will help them to feel safe and protected. Recognising fears and apprehensions shown by children towards people or situations that causes them to be anxious or nervous might indicate abuse particularly sexual abuse. A child may choose to talk to a trusted adult about abuse. Whilst communication plays a significant role in disclosure, practitioners who are 'tuned in' to children will also learn to read the more subtle signals from children indicating that all is not well.

• Knowledge of parents, family members and significant adults in the life of a child.

Understanding family contexts, relationships and how they impact upon children is important. Relationships with parents, siblings and extended family members or other significant adults in the child's life should be considered when understanding the bigger picture. Children may spend lots of time with wider family members such as grandparents, cousins or stepbrothers and sisters. Children who move between or reside in different households will naturally encounter lots of people other than their own parents. This can sometimes broaden the risks to children especially if parents are less able to provide protective factors for them. Practitioners should be aware of new or restored relationships that parents develop between themselves and intimate partners, particularly if they are spending time with the child.

• Being aware of changes to a child's living arrangements.

With an increasing amount of housing uncertainty for families and a significant rise in homelessness, risks to children go far beyond those of the emotional upheaval of moving house and the anxieties and stress that this may cause. Many families and children who are deemed homeless will be living in temporary accommodation such as hostels or bed and breakfast residences that could exposes them to risk of abuse by others who are living there also.

• Creating opportunities and encouraging children to be emotionally literate.

Helping children to recognise and communicate their feelings is important for lots of reasons. I visited a nursery where the manager explained her intent in creating an environment where children could express their feelings and communicate with skilful practitioners who would listen and respond to them. The culture evident across the setting of listening and tuning into children's feelings was having a tremendous impact upon children in a really positive way. Children used picture cards to describe emotions and were encouraged to talk about a range of feelings. Interactions between adults and children helped explore how they felt inside. Maidstone-Cotton (2021) talks about the 'importance of beginning to use emotion language with children from babyhood, by embedding it in our work'. By doing so this provides the 'important tools they can use throughout their life'. By encouraging emotional literacy in young children, practitioners can help with the language they need to communicate that something might be wrong.

- Helping children to understand body privacy and building confidence in them to speak out if they are uncomfortable about someone or a situation.

Talking about body privacy with young children provides opportunities to address a number of things. Not only are we instilling messages that make clear expectations and boundaries in relation to children's bodies belonging to them and them having the right to privacy, but we are offering an empowerment and confidence for children to stand up for themselves if they feel awkward or uneasy about actions towards them from others. Teaching children to adhere to privacy etiquette not only enables them to develop respectful and considerate relationships with each other but it has the potential to contribute towards building protective factors in children that keep them safe from sexual predators.
Things to consider about body parts and privacy:

- Views and perspectives on nudity may vary from one family to another.
- Talking about private parts such as male and female genitalia may be openly discussed in families with children using the correct names and terminology whilst some families will avoid talking about it and use words or nick names, a descriptive name given to the body part instead of the real name.
- Children from an early age should be provided with opportunities to undertake intimate care practices such as nappy changing, using the toilet or undressing in places where their privacy is protected.

- Children should be taught to make their own decisions about whether they want others touching them, kissing them, or offering hugs and physical contact without their invitation or wanting to do so.
- Boundaries should be set in relation to inappropriate touching of intimate areas on a child's body.

    Children should be taught to distinguish the difference between appropriate touch and inappropriate touch. This can be skilfully supported by adults. As children are helped at home or in their early years setting to go to the toilet, to undress and wash by a trusted adult or when they might be examined by a medical professional, they can be reassured that this is acceptable. Children need to learn the difference between this type of touch and inappropriate touch such as exploratory play between other children or, most concerning, children or adults whose motives are sinister and abusive towards them.

- Children need to learn that it's not ok for someone else to show them their intimate body parts, or to ask them to touch them whether they are another child or adult, and whether they know them or don't know them.
- Children should learn the difference between keeping secrets about special events or surprises and those that are secrets asked to be kept by someone who is doing something to them that is harmful and abusive.

We don't like to talk about sexual abuse

I remember working in a community where significant and historical sexual abuse had taken place over a period of time. This community was also very much defined by its faith and beliefs and some, including local religious leaders, refused to accept that sexual abuse happened at all. If it did, they were not prepared to acknowledge it as such, actively finding ways to hide it and keep it a secret. I was asked to deliver safeguarding training by a community group on the premise that we would not mention sexual abuse as this would offend the audience. The denial that this type of abuse could never happen within this faith community was very much part of a sinister and troubling response from those who knew it was happening and should have reported the crimes to the police. We absolutely must talk about sexual abuse, however unpleasant, and we must begin to talk about inappropriate, intimate touching and privacy, not to make children fearful or scared rather to offer both preventative and responsive strategies that safeguard young children.

Of all four categories, *neglect* remains the highest and main reason as to why a child will be assessed by social care followed in order by *emotional abuse, physical abuse* and *sexual abuse.*

TIME TO REFLECT

If you are working independently as a childminder or nanny, think about the situations where the defence of child abuse or neglect might occur because of different cultural responses to abuse. Use the statements in the next section to reflect on this.

TEAM TALK

Take some time within your team to talk about how society or different cultures normalise child abuse or neglect, making it seem acceptable or excusing it as something that inevitably happens to children rather than identifying it as being abusive or neglectful. How do we view the following statements and how do we respond to them?

> *Neglect* – 'it's to be expected within certain families'.
> *Emotional abuse* – 'he's being oversensitive and needs to learn to toughen up'.
> *Physical abuse* – 'well I was smacked as a child, it never hurt me'.
> *Sexual abuse* – 'they were teenagers consenting to sex with older men so that's not abuse'.

TIME TO THINK

How does the normalisation of child abuse and neglect detract from what it really is? How has this formed your own perceptions and views of safeguarding and child protection?

Figure 2.1   Places where I feel safe, at home, school and when I'm at gymnastics.

Key messages from chapter two

- Understanding the definitions of abuse and neglect helps early years practitioners to identify harm and take appropriate actions.
- Recognising abuse and neglect and its impact young children is a vital and most important feature of effective safeguarding and child protection practice.
- Abuse and neglect can occur in the lives of children regardless of their economic or social status.
- Child abuse is prevalent in all areas of society and younger children are significantly vulnerable.
- Effective strategies developed and applied in practice by an early year's workforce can safeguard and protect children.

References

Bernard, C. (2018). *An Exploration of How Social Workers Engage Neglectful Parents from Affluent Backgrounds in the Child Protection System.* Goldsmiths, University of London.

Bywaters, P., Bunting, L., Davidson, G., Hanratty, J., Mason, W., McCartan, C., and Steils, N. (2016). *The Relationship Between Poverty, Child Abuse and Neglect: An Evidence Review.* Joseph Rowntree Foundation.

Greater Manchester Safeguarding. *5.2.3 Bruising Protocol for Immobile Babies and Children* (proceduresonline.com).

HM Gov. (2015). *What to Do If You Are Worried a Child is Being Abused. Advice for Practitioners.* HM Gov.

HM Gov. (2018). *Working Together to Safeguard Children. A Guide to Inter Agency Working to Safeguard and Promote the Welfare of Children.* HM Gov.

Joseph Rowntree Foundation. (2021). *UK Poverty 2020/21.* JRF.

Maidstone-Cotton, S. (2021). *Supporting Children with Social, Emotional and Mental Health Needs in the Early Years: Practical Solutions and Strategies for Every Setting.* London and New York: Routledge.

National Guidance for Child Protection in Scotland. (2021). Scottish Government (gov.scot).

Wigan Safeguarding Partnership. *Injuries in Non-mobile Children* (wiganlscb. com) (Accessed 20.6.22).

3 | The role of the designated safeguarding lead

The role of the lead practitioner for safeguarding and child protection in early years settings is of course one of the most important features of effective safeguarding practice. They take on a range of responsibilities that impact upon children in their setting. If you are currently undertaking this role or are one of a number of leads in your setting, such as a deputy or room leader, this chapter will be of great significance to you. For those aspiring to become leaders in the future, or those who work alongside the safeguarding lead, an understanding of the requirements and functions within the role are vital.

This represents the **manage** element of the overall process that is mentioned in earlier chapters as **identify, help, protect** and **manage.**

Manage – refers to the processes that primarily fall upon leaders and managers whose remit it is to take a lead role to safeguard and protect children. The management elements in this whole process can also involve a range of things.

Such as:

- Management oversight, including creating policies and establishing effective systems and procedures.
- Liaising with outside agencies including statutory services.
- Record keeping and sharing information.

For those working in settings with one or more members of staff it may include:

- Safer recruitment.
- Supervision of staff and managing the ongoing suitability of the workforce.
- Developing their own and others safeguarding skills and knowledge.

DOI: 10.4324/9781003137054-3

Whose role is it anyway?

It is fair to say that the early years sector has a diverse range of people for whom the role of safeguarding lead is both relevant and applicable. The role includes managers and deputy managers of **day-care settings, sessional care** including **out of school provision** and **creches, childminders** and **nannies.** Maintained nurseries or schools will most likely recognise the head teacher as their designated safeguarding lead. The role may vary depending on the person undertaking it, but the fundamental factors that enable effective practice to take place are always centred on the needs of children.

TIME TO REFLECT

If you are a safeguarding lead for your setting, think about the range of responsibilities and tasks associated with this role. If you are not the lead, you might want to note what you know about the role from observing others.

The three C's and the designated safeguarding lead

We have established that all leads may take on differing roles depending on their setting and the context in which they work. As simple or complex as this may be, the following areas summarise the important elements that go towards being an effective designated safeguarding lead. In brief, leads should be **COMPLIANT, COMPETENT** and **CONFIDENT**.

Compliant

In a sector that is directed and governed by legislation, the basis upon which we develop practice must be that of compliance. It is the primary building block upon which we construct sound and effective safeguarding practices that meet desired outcomes for children and adults with whom we work. Being compliant is the minimum requirement that a designated lead must meet and is therefore our starting point. Legislation reflects requirements that we are expected to adhere to and work with. Working with children for many years, I am old enough to remember when a number of key legislative changes came into place and more importantly why and what led to their development. Legislation usually emerges from a place that recognises the need to address a situation and/or change something that needs reform.

In England, for instance, the emphasis upon **The Children Act (1989)** was largely driven by the need not only to review and change childcare law for those working within it but most importantly for children and families for whom it was intended. The key principles underpinning this Act centre on the child. For example, this law notes the 'primary responsibility for the upbringing of children rests with families' (Ryan 1999). It emphasises the importance of race, culture and language and led to a shift in focus so that children became central to processes undertaken by local authorities. Expectations of this Act are that children will be spoken with and consulted; their wishes and feelings have to be taken into account particularly where decisions about them are being made. Whilst partnership and multi-agency work featured in the 1989 Act, the emphasis upon a greater and more proactive approach to deliver multi-agency practice came later through **The Children Act (2004)**. This Act was driven by the tragedy of Victoria Climbie in 2000 and acted upon the findings of Lord Laming, who was the author of the public enquiry into her death. The 2004 Act reinforced the safeguarding responsibilities of all people and organisations working with children.

Legislation that underpins effective safeguarding and child protection practices enables us to fulfil a number of requirements.

- Upholding children's rights to be heard, seen and protected.
- Keeping children physically and emotionally safe and well.
- Always promoting children's wellbeing.
- Recognising individual responsibilities and the collective responsibilities of others such as statutory services or specialist support from those with whom we work.

Legislation guides and assists practitioners to fulfil the following functions.

- Adhere to health and safety laws.
- Share personal and sensitive information.

- Meet children's individual needs in respect to diversity and inclusion, promoting equality for all.
- It compels us to take appropriate action.

Frameworks such as the **Early Years Foundation Stage** (England) are a legal requirement and should be seen as such. Practitioners working in England and registered to deliver childcare under **The Childcare Act (2006)** therefore have a duty to meet these requirements. The 'MUST have' or the 'MUST do' noted in the text in this framework signifies what is legally expected and must be followed as such, in turn demonstrating practitioners' compliance.

Government guidance whilst not in the same context as legal frameworks are underpinned by legislation. Child protection or safeguarding statutory guidance for England, Scotland, Wales and Northern Ireland will a have a legislative basis upon which guidance has to be adopted in each country.

In comparing various frameworks and their underpinning legislation it is easy to recognise familiar emphasis and supporting standards upon which governments have established expectations for practice and enabling interventions that place children's best interests at the heart of all that they seek to achieve and do.

TIME TO THINK AND TEAM TALK

Considering the legislative and governmental directives that early year's practitioners work towards, identify those that apply to you and how these are delivered within your own local context. If you work in a team discuss with colleagues and write a list of directives that you adhere to in practice.

Devolved powers in all four nations of England have resulted in various legislative and governmental directives.

Wales

Key underpinning legislation

Social Services and Well-being (Wales) Act 2014.

Government guidance

Working Together to Safeguard People: Code of Safeguarding Practice (2022).
    This Welsh statutory guidance refers to the 'code of safeguarding practice', setting out Welsh Government expectations in relation to safeguarding arrangements for individuals, groups or organisations delivering activities or services to children.

Scotland

Key underpinning legislation

The Children Act (Scotland) 1995.
    The Children and Young People Act (Scotland) 2014.

Government guidance and national frameworks

* National guidance for child protection in Scotland.
* The Getting it right for every child framework (GIRFEC).

The GIRFEC framework incorporates the SHANARRI wellbeing indicators, recognises what it is that children need for the best start in life and identifies the important elements that enable them to achieve success. SHANARRI stands for safe, healthy, achieving, nurtured, active, respected, responsible and included.

Northern Ireland

Key underpinning legislation

The Children Order (Northern Ireland) 1995.

This legislation is the main statute for the governance of care, upbringing and protection of children in Northern Ireland.

Government guidance and national frameworks

Co-operating to safeguard children 2017.

The guidance sets out the roles and responsibilities for practitioners working with children in Northern Ireland, making clear the expectations to protect children from abuse or neglect.

We should not approach our duties to be compliant reluctantly or think of legislation as something that is restrictive or with anxiety should we get it wrong. We should instead consider legislation and the need to be compliant as empowering practitioners to abide by laws that are deep rooted in principles and values that are central to children's wellbeing and safety.

TIME TO REFLECT

What legislation and Government guidance, including those noted in the previous sections. should you be aware of that will underpin your actions and decision making in the following scenarios?

Scenario 1

A child who attends your setting is presenting with poor hygiene and you are concerned that health checks and regular appointments are not being kept. You need to establish the bigger picture by gaining information from other agencies about their involvement with the child to inform your decisions about a potential referral to social care.

Scenario 2

A mother of three-year-old twins confides in you that she is the victim of domestic abuse. She explains that her partner, not the children's father, controls everything in relation to the family home and income. He also times her going to and from dropping off the children at the setting, checking her mobile phone to see who is messaging and calling her. Ongoing conflict and tensions between mom and her partner are making the children anxious and afraid. Mom asks you not to tell anyone about the abuse for fear of reprisal from her partner.

Designated safeguarding leads should be COMPLIANT.

Competent

Whilst legislative frameworks and government guidance offer some detail of what a designated safeguarding lead is required to achieve, there really are no set-in-stone competencies to guide us. I want to consider some overarching themes that feature some of the main competencies I believe are necessary for those taking safeguarding and child protection lead responsibilities in early years settings. Within these competencies I have included qualities, skills and abilities.

Qualities of the designated safeguarding lead

Leadership qualities are vitally important and underpin the way in which leaders and managers operate within their roles.

These are some of the qualities that effective safeguarding leads require:

- They selflessly prioritise children in all that they do and adopt professionally curious approaches to understand what is happening for a child.
- They show and demonstrate empathy.
- They are good listeners and communicators.
- They are tenacious in their desire to achieve the right outcomes for children and families.
- They are intuitive, recognising that intuition contributes to other relevant factors that help to establish facts.
- They work calmly and professionally in times of crisis.
- They remain focussed on the child and recognise factors that influence or distract from keeping children safe and well and act to combat them.
- They demonstrate uncompromising resolve in their plight to keep children safe and well.
- They can acknowledge and recognise the need to keep themselves and their own wellbeing intact.

- They are reflective practitioners.
- They recognise the importance of and undertake their responsibilities in providing good role models to children, parents, staff and others with whom they work.

Essential skills for the designated safeguarding lead

Knowledge is key

Safeguarding leads are required to have sufficient and appropriate knowledge of safeguarding and child protection. This means that they should be able to recognise signs of abuse and neglect and respond appropriately. More so they need to understand the unique elements of risks that present to young children, which in turn helps them determine the consequences or impact of such risks upon the child. We know that children under twelve months of age account for most of all children needing protection. This surely brings home the urgency and importance of upskilling and equipping practitioners working in the early years to be super effective in their roles. Younger children need us to advocate for them more so than older children due to their additional vulnerabilities and their inability to communicate. Leads therefore must acquire skills that identify both the subtle and sometimes complex signs of abuse and neglect.

What do we need to know?

It is important to approach our attainment of safeguarding knowledge not merely as an information gathering exercise. To be knowledgeable or well informed involves both information and skill. The basis of safeguarding knowledge should be derived from education and experience. Safeguarding knowledge cannot therefore be simply reduced to learning a check list of themes or topics that practitioners believe might provide them with sufficient information about the things related to safeguarding and child protection so that they can be effective safeguarding leads.

It concerns me greatly that, over time, the early years sector has often become pre-occupied with seeking knowledge about safeguarding and child protection to provide the correct responses for the regulator rather than for the benefit of children with whom they work. This approach to learning that focusses on second guessing an inspector's enquiry or questions about safeguarding and being able to answer questions by rote is unhelpful. It removes the child from being the primary focus. Our determination and motivation to obtain knowledge must be driven alone by the desire to safeguard and protect children.

A worried childminder once approached me during training to tell me that an Ofsted inspector had asked her what she knew about breast ironing. She had to admit to the inspector that she didn't know what this was and was anxious that this would have negative consequences on the outcome of her inspection. This childminder was experienced and knowledgeable, but she didn't know about breast ironing. We took time as part of the wider training to explore what as early years practitioners we did know rather than worrying about those things we did not know. We discussed practitioners' deep knowledge of children who are seen regularly and consistently in settings, knowledge about parents and wider family members. Consideration to local safeguarding and child protection priorities identified by the town's Local Safeguarding Partnership were discussed. We drew upon learning from published reviews noting particular focus on injuries in non-mobile children and we explored how we might identify children who are experiencing domestic abuse given the large numbers of reports known in the local authority. We established when and how actions should be taken.

The important thing to remember about safeguarding knowledge is that we will always have something new to learn. Having sufficient and relevant knowledge means that practitioners will know how to identify concerns, be able to put this into context and respond in the right way.

Being reflective

Reflective practitioners will be able to identify what knowledge they require and how they will achieve this. Furthermore, they will understand the need to keep knowledge updated and relevant to their roles and the children and families they work with. Self-directed learning, in other words taking responsibility for our own learning, plays a significant part in how the designated safeguarding lead approaches and fulfils their learning goals.

The designated safeguarding lead knowledge toolkit

Having established that knowledge informs and precedes our responses to act on behalf of a child, there are some essential and helpful knowledge descriptors that every designated safeguarding lead should have available to them in their knowledge toolkit.

Here are some suggestions.

Knowledge essentials

- Identifying and recognising signs of abuse and neglect and how they impact upon children.
- Understanding child development including brain development and what undermines healthy development for children especially in the first five years of life.
- Identification and recognition of factors that adversely impact upon children from both within their family contexts and within an extra familial context (outside of their family). Knowing how to be 'alert to issues in the life of a child at home or elsewhere', which in turn helps to identify risks for children (DfE 2021).
- Knowledge of an individual child's life experiences, family contexts, protective factors, ongoing circumstances and relationships with other adults, their lived experiences and how this may affect them.
- Understanding levels of need – thresholds that determine the level of need for each child as defined by local authorities' threshold of need guidance or equivalent.
- How to respond to a child's need for early help (early intervention) and how to engage with local procedures for assessment, contributing to plans and engaging in targeted interventions for a child.
- Knowledge of the local authority children's social care team, the name and contact details of the team for example the Multi-Agency Safeguarding Hub (MASH) or equivalent. Knowing how to effectively liaise with them and their procedures on safeguarding and child protection matters.
- Knowledge of local authority priorities and bespoke elements that define responses to safeguarding themes within their geographic area and as determined by Local Safeguarding Partners or other local authority bodies with strategic responsibilities and oversight for child protection.
- How to take actions for children who are in immediate danger of harm including contacting the Police or Children's Services Social Care.
- Understanding risks to children that occur because of professional abuse and knowing how to respond and follow procedures. This includes how to contact and report to the Local Authority Designated Safeguarding Officer (LADO) or other bodies who are responsible to investigate allegations of harm against children from professionals or adults who work with them.
- How to make a referral to social care in respect of a child at risk of significant harm.

(Continued)

(Continued)

Knowledge essentials

- Understanding the processes and procedures that follow assessment of need and the role that early year's providers play in respect to their involvement for multi-agency plans and interventions. This includes how these are monitored, reviewed and the role that leads will take in making decisions.
- Understanding the importance of effective record keeping and knowing how to effectively record, maintain records and use them skilfully to write and produce reports.
- Knowledge of the legal basis for gathering, storing and sharing of information about a child and using this to underpin effective information sharing and safeguarding practices.
- Being knowledgeable of relevant legislative contexts and know how to fulfil and meet their legal requirements in practice.
- How to respond and meet expectations of Government guidance in respect to undertaking their responsibilities to safeguard and protect children. Acquiring knowledge from Government guidance to gain understanding of the responsibilities of others they work alongside, including the role of multi-agency practices and the functions of statutory services.
- Knowledge of local procedures that enable engagement in processes that escalate concerns for children to challenge other practitioners' decision making or practice if it is believed not to be in the best interests of the child.
- How to respond to a child's disclosure.
- Where to signpost adults with whom they work to services that offer them help and support.

Knowledge essentials for leads supporting or managing other staff

- How to implement safer recruitment processes and procedures.
- Understanding the importance and rationale for ongoing staff suitability. Being able to undertake suitability checks and processes including how to report to the disclosure and barring services or equivalent where appropriate.
- How to lead, support and develop staff in equipping them to recognise and respond to abuse and neglect.
- Knowledge of what makes for effective management systems that safeguard and protect children in their setting. Leaders will draw upon their knowledge to create, implement and update policies and reviews of procedures ensuring that they are effective and in keeping with local safeguarding arrangements within their local authority.
- Knowledge of how to implement and maintain excellent management oversight that focusses on children and their needs. Including formal systems that enable good recording and reporting practices.
- Understanding and being able to conduct effective professional supervision and how this achieves a team wide approach in facilitating recognition of concerns for children and responding appropriately.

TIME TO REFLECT

How confident do you feel in fulfilling the knowledge essentials in the designated safeguarding lead toolkit? Where you have identified areas for development how might you gain or upskill your essential knowledge and what or who might this involve?

Training

Competent staff, whether the designated safeguarding lead or otherwise, will achieve levels of competency through training. The Early Years Foundation makes clear expectations about training for practitioners working in England. It states that the 'lead practitioner must attend a child protection training course that enables them to identify, understand and respond appropriately to signs of possible abuse and neglect' (DfE 2021). The requirement to take account of 'any advice from the Local Safeguarding Partner or local authority on appropriate training courses' is sometimes overlooked by practitioners. Once again, the relevance of this narrative reminds us of the importance of working within local contexts, making us aware of priorities and objectives that have been identified and agreed by governing bodies and those responsible for safeguarding and child protection in our local areas. Where advice and direction are given by local authorities about specific training, this enables specific focus on the needs of children and families with whom we are directly working with. Training should take place on a regular basis and knowledge should be consistently and frequently updated.

Keeping up with emergent themes

It makes sense to consider competencies that are intrinsically linked to training as an excellent means by which we can extend learning and develop new or build upon existing skills. Whilst not advocating that it is necessary to know everything possible about safeguarding and child protection to be competent leads, it is important to keep up to date with current learning and evidence-based research that informs our roles. This can be done by accessing training courses or reading research and reports written by experts in their field. There are two areas that have emerged more recently that are worth noting.

Adverse Childhood Experiences – ACEs

In recent years there has been a growing attention for practitioners to understand the impact of trauma upon children and adults alike, because of adverse childhood experiences. Trauma informed practice, understanding how to respond to children who have experienced abuse or neglect, is essential to meet the needs of some of the most vulnerable children in our care. Competent designated safeguarding leads will consider how practice in their setting supports children who have experienced or who are continuing to experience childhood trauma. Along with other successful pedagogical approaches in the early years, practice that supports the holistic needs of the child are vital. We will refer further to the effects of adverse childhood experiences (ACEs) in chapters 4 and 6.

Contextual safeguarding – assessment of risk outside of the family home

Contextual safeguarding considers the wider factors of risk and assessment of risk for children experiencing abuse from outside of the family environment. These risks are often referred to as extra-familial risks or threats and recognise that some 'children may be vulnerable to abuse or exploitation from outside their families' (HM Gov 2018). Contextual safeguarding highlights the developments of substantial changes in society that challenge our perceptions of wider risks to children. Risks such as child-on-child abuse, online harms, or dangers in their wider community. Whilst extra-familial risks feature highly in the lives of older children, the impact upon all children, young and old, is significant and must be understood by those working with them. A further exploration of extra-familial risks to children in the early years can be found in chapter 4.

Learning from case reviews

One of the main objectives that arise from undertaking and publishing case reviews is the spotlight on learning they provide. Whilst they prove a difficult read due to the in-depth detail of child abuse and neglect, they offer an important overview and understanding on the risks and all too frequent failings in child protection practice. Using such reviews to inform and build upon our knowledge as designated safeguarding leads is therefore helpful. They provide early years practitioners with several key features:

- Recognises personalised risks to younger children.
- Highlights the extent of re-occurring themes such as

  - poor information sharing,
  - lack of joined up thinking and shared working,
  - lack of professional curiosity,
  - failure to see, understand and act upon the child's lived experiences.

- Identifies specific vulnerabilities within certain groups of people and takes changing circumstances for children into account.
- Characterises specific dangers known to children in a local geographical area.
- Reminds us of the need to be susceptible and respond to all abuse regardless of family status or circumstance.

Safeguarding practice reviews or equivalent are not meant to apportion blame to any one individual or organisation working with children and their families. The scrutinising elements of reviews do however show where things have tragically gone wrong. Learning from such reviews helps all practitioners to reflect on the learning and apply this to their own practices.

Knowledge and experience

There are lots of advantages that come from having first-hand experience of working with children and families who need help and protection. Experience provides practitioners with the scope to draw upon familiar recognition of safeguarding concerns and results in acquiring the direct know-hows of practice and procedures that follow a concern. Designated safeguarding leads who have significant experience in terms of scope and longevity in the role are a much-needed source of support to children. Lack of experience does not however render leads as ineffective when it comes to safeguarding.

I have supported a network of childminders in my hometown, delivering training to them for the past ten years. Every time we meet, usually every two years or so, a small number in the group tell me that they have never needed to engage with processes such as challenging parents about their child's well-being or making a referral to social care in all the time that they have worked as childminders. They still ensure that they engage in training regularly and actively seek updated information relevant to their roles. This investment builds upon their safeguarding practice competencies. The dilemmas of having little or no safeguarding experience is a common theme for childminders and nannies often due to the small numbers of children with whom they work. There are however many home-based childcare practitioners who have frequent opportunities to use their personal experiences as a means by which to build and extend their knowledge and skills. Experience is not always essential, but knowledge is the key factor that contributes towards making the right decisions in respect of a child's wellbeing and safety.

TIME TO REFLECT

Think about your latest safeguarding training. What was the most significant thing that you learnt from the training, whether new information or a realisation of a concept or strategy that you had not previously thought about?

How do you keep your safeguarding knowledge up to date?

Effective management

Let us return to consider the knowledge essentials for leads supporting or managing other staff, particularly in the context of effective management skills and oversight. I fully take on board that this may vary from one setting to another and have tried to make these examples of management competencies applicable to most. The basis of management oversight is reflected in the simple strategies put into place and overseen by leads and do not need to be complicated or cumbersome. If you are responsible for others in your workplace, no matter the size or number of your team as a safeguarding lead, there are some questions you may wish to ask yourself and reflect upon. This will help you to consider the key issues of effective lead management.

- Does everyone know how to recognise and respond to abuse and neglect in my setting?
- Do staff have an ongoing working knowledge of the setting's policies and procedures?
- Are systems in place that enable reporting concerns about a child, including those relating to staff conduct and behaviours?
- Do all staff, students, regular visitors and/or volunteers know who the designated safeguarding leads are and do they understand the role and how they are expected to work with them?
- Do staff and adults working in the setting always have access to the designated safeguarding lead or deputy named lead? Does an open-door policy provide a listening culture in the setting that acts upon concerns about children?
- Is communication in the setting enabling? Does it allow a free flow of information that supports professional judgements and decision making whilst maintaining appropriate confidentialities?
- Are managers and leaders working in a transparent manner demonstrating their openness to challenge and scrutiny by those they work with?
- Are staff empowered to know where to take concerns about non- or poor reporting and whistleblowing to others outside of their organisation or workplace?

The National Society for the Prevention of Cruelty to Children (NSPCC) reported on key findings gathered from case reviews with recognised early years sector involvement in child protection. The report (2021), which placed significant emphasis on the need for greater management oversight and responsibility, determined four key issues that needed to be addressed to improve child protection practice in the early years.

1. Practitioners need a better understanding of how to *'recognise'* and *'respond'* to child protection concerns.
2. Early years practitioners should 'build up a picture of a *'child's lived experience'* and to apply *'professional curiosity'* about a child's life outside of the setting'.
3. Staff should engage in *'regular'* and *'ongoing'* effective *'child protection training'*. Managers should have *'sufficient oversight of practice'* and should 'engage in *reflective supervision* with practitioners'.
4. Child protection leads should know with whom to *'share information'* and be able to *'follow local escalation procedures'* if they consider appropriate action is not being taken by other agencies.

Management oversight is fundamental to effective safeguarding practices that centre on the child's wellbeing and safety.

Designated safeguarding leads should be COMPETENT.

Confident

Confidence often takes time to grow and develop.

I remember the sense of immense responsibility when I began work as a nursery officer for a local authority run, social services day nursery in the 1990s. I was concerned about what would happen if I got things wrong. I was under confident. Of course, like others who are beginning their journey into something new, I did make mistakes. Sometimes I misunderstood contexts or lacked the knowledge to understand a situation as best as I probably could have. What did help was being able to work alongside experienced colleagues who had been in the role a lot longer than I had. This meant that I could draw upon their knowledge and learn from them. It is always helpful to take advice from those who are more experienced; likewise it is important for experienced practitioners to reach out to others to support their learning. One thing that I have noted both from personal experience and as I observe others is that our approach to learning that builds confidence as designated safeguarding leads is two-fold.

1. It needs to be proactive and driven by the individual, reflecting and recognising what we need to know and why.
2. It needs to develop organically through on-the-job experiences that we can draw upon, making us confident practitioners.

Coincidentally, as I write this chapter, I am contacted by a childminder of twelve years who has for the first time needed to engage with services due a safeguarding concern with one of the children in her setting. 'I just need to check I'm doing the right thing as I've not had to do this before' she told me. She needed someone to reassure her. She had done the right thing and followed policy and procedure correctly. When it comes to engaging with safeguarding practices, confidence or under confidence contributes substantially to the process. A confident practitioner will drive forward the process that focusses on the child, ensuring safe and protective outcomes for them. An under confident practitioner may be hesitant, contributing to delays in actions taken to protect a child. Their uncertainty or feelings of insecurity both personally and regarding a situation may result in poor outcomes for children. Confidence is key if we are to be determined to act on behalf of children who themselves are unable to speak out and change a situation for the better.

Designated safeguarding leads engage in a whole range of things to safeguard children where confidence is essential.

Making professional judgements

My understanding of making professional judgements, and the context in which I apply this phrase, refers to judgements made by practitioners that draw upon knowledge and understanding of a person, child or/and a situation. To make professional judgements, which are a necessary function of a confident lead, they will require information that helps them to analyse a situation, discern or establish what is happening or likely to happen.

I frequently find myself encouraging leads to consider their contributions towards making judgements as being more significant than they or others might believe them to be. A childminder is told by a parent that this is 'just their opinion' on a matter of considerable concern for a child. A manager of a nursery attending a child protection conference is encouraged by other professionals to reconsider their scoring of levels of danger for the child because, ultimately, they would like to close the case. Confident leads will stay firm and make professional judgements, trusting in their knowledge of the child, in what they understand and know because they see the child and work with the family frequently and consistently.

Some further considerations about making professional judgements:

- All professionals working with children have an equal role when making judgements.
- Always be prepared to re-visit your judgements especially if new or other relevant information comes to light.

Making decisions

Decision making when in the context of safeguarding and child protection requires various level of confidence.

We make decisions about lots of things:

- When to raise concerns in respect of a child's injury, disclosure of abuse or neglect and talk to parents about this.
- When to engage other professionals in sharing and seeking information about a child.
- Acting to seek advice from other professionals on something we are not sure about.
- Acknowledging levels of need for a child and making decisions in respect to interventions that should happen to achieve positive outcomes.
- Initiating assessment for early help or a referral to social care.
- Whether to escalate or de-escalate the needs of a child.

Sometime decisions can be made independently and won't involve anyone else. Having colleagues to help us with decision making is extremely beneficial and empowering especially if there is some uncertainty surrounding the decision. Collaborative decision making in the context of multi-agency practice is therefore highly effective, particularly when all who are involved are determined to place the child at the centre of all they consider and conclude.

We will refer to processes that inform and lead to taking decisive action in chapter 5.

Being confident to challenge

Challenge is an important part of effective safeguarding practice. It may involve calling upon a person to explain or substantiate something that we are suspicious about. A parent who cannot understand the detrimental effect of their actions or behaviours upon their child, or a parent who gives an inconsistent account of how their child has received an injury, both require challenge. Situations that require inquisitive interactions between practitioners and parents can be difficult and involve various levels of confidence depending on the reason for the challenge and how confident they may be is in undertaking the task. Gentle challenge, for instance such as introducing the notion that a lack of understanding from a parent is leading to the problem, can be easy to accomplish. Challenge that involves confrontation however is very different. Challenging someone who appears to be deceptive, manipulative and actively disregarding the safety or wellbeing of their child will inevitably involve confrontation. Challenge in this instance is difficult and will generate a sense of hostility. Few people like confrontation but it is sometimes a much-needed strategy that aids professionally curiosity. Confident leads will press for clarification on matters of concern and often expose undesirable truths about child abuse or neglect.

Challenge in the role of safeguarding lead may involve addressing a safeguarding concern about a colleague or staff team member.

The need for professional challenge is a regular and reoccurring theme. Leads should be confident to know when and how to challenge other professionals they work with if they believe this is necessary. Professional challenge is appropriate for lots of reasons or circumstances:

- Not sharing information about a child or family.
- Excluding early years practitioners from multi-agency processes including minutes for meetings and not asking for representation at such meetings.
- Lack of recognition from other professionals regarding early years practitioners' responsibilities that safeguard and protect children.
- Disputing the levels of need for a child as defined by local authority thresholds.
- Not accepting referrals for services (including statutory services) if the child's needs are appropriate for them to do so.

- Demonstrating a lack of child-centred practice or approach to safeguarding for children and families with whom they work.

Being confident to challenge other professionals is necessary as we navigate our way around multi-agency engagement and practices. Leads should be able to both challenge others and to receive challenge where appropriate themselves. Challenge should open up the idea that we could do things differently or reflect on different perspectives including our own practices.

Case reviews frequently draw upon learning that concludes practitioners need to know how to challenge decision making that is not in the best interests of the child. Designated safeguarding leads should know how to escalate concerns and be confident to do so.

Designated safeguarding leads should be CONFIDENT.

TIME TO REFLECT

Compliant – What child-centred practices do you recognise within the legislation that underpins your safeguarding responsibilities in the early years?

Competent – What do you consider are the main features of a competent lead and what makes you capable to fulfil your role?

Confident – How confident are you in your role as lead? How can you build confidence given your personal experiences and circumstances within your setting?

In practice – what designated safeguarding leads say about their role in the early years

Help and support

'Working in areas of high deprivation has its challenges. As DSL I have benefited from the advice of the local authority safeguarding lead who is always at the end of the phone to help with any problems.'

Learning to be confident

'Child protection conferences initially seemed daunting to attend but as I gained experience and confidence, I found it less stressful. I have worked with some wonderful Independent Reviewing Officers whose knowledge and expertise amazes me. I have been able to glean aspects of my own knowledge through them.'

Leadership models that effectively facilitate the role of the designated safeguarding lead

Early years leadership is distinct and is rooted in pedagogical principles that are centred on the holistic needs of children. It is therefore helpful to consider the wider approaches that are needed for safeguarding leads when working with young children and their families. A reflective lead not only will recognise the expectations of their role, but they will acknowledge how they work or operate as an effective leader. They will consider personal characteristics, styles and methodologies that offer optimum results as they advocate on behalf of children.

Child-centred safeguarding and child protection practice draws upon more than one leadership model.

Collaborative leadership both recognises and operates in a way that actively embraces and engages others to fulfil recognised objectives for children. Siraj-Blatchford and Manni (2007) states that *'Leadership within the early years sector concerns relational leadership, groups of people collaboratively working together to complete tasks and goals rather than being the work of one leader'*. This style of leadership is essential when working in a multi-agency context.

Directional leadership demonstrated through the role of the designated safeguarding lead offers a strong focus on vision and purpose that is evident across a wider group of people. Siraj-Blatchford and Hallet (2014) believe the 'ability for a leader to develop and articulate a shared vision is central to directional leadership.' They consider this model of leadership provides a 'purposeful pathway for policy, provision and practice' in early years settings. This style of leadership delivers a clear expectation and steer for others to follow and engage with.

Distributed leadership models feature a shared responsibility and recognition that leadership duties and roles can be issued by the lead to one or more people under their supervision. Whilst there are elements of distributed leadership that are suitable for designated leads to allocate, it is important that deployment of tasks should be both proportionate and appropriate. Harris (2002) describes the 'main advantage of distributed leadership is that it increases the level of skills and expertise available'. This style of leadership means that the wider benefits of equipping a competent and resourceful team of practitioners will serve to increase the potential to respond and act with greater effect. It emphasises the point that safeguarding children does not rely on one person alone.

Emotional intelligence

Emotionally intelligent pedagogical leadership is at the heart of child-centred practice. Leaders who are emotionally intelligent will display attributes noted by Goleman (1996). They will:

- Be able to manage their own emotions.
- Have a sense of empathy.
- Be able to repair emotional damage in themselves and others.
- Be emotionally interactive – that is, tuning into people so that they can interact with them effectively.

Managing big emotions

It goes without saying that the emotional aspects when engaging in features of safeguarding and protecting children are hugely significant. Working in a sector that is motivated by the desire to care and nurture young children can be difficult for us when we witness first-hand child abuse or neglect. The range of emotions that this evokes in us are wide and varied. We may feel sadness, grief and an overwhelming sense of despair on behalf of a child we work with. We may experience anger directed towards perpetrators of abuse or despair when we struggle to get a desired resolve for a child that needs someone to act and intervene on their behalf. All of these and more are the big emotions that come with the responsibilities of lead role for safeguarding and child pro-tection; how we manage and process this is important. Recognising how we are feeling and acknowledging our emotions is necessary. To deny or ignore emotional responses would be unhelpful and in fact counterproductive in our objectives to make a difference or change a situation where possible.

Recognising and being able to manage the big emotions demonstrates a level of *emotional competency* in safeguarding leads. They will be able to acknowledge many important and essential aspects that arise from being emo-tionally adept and competent.

- It is important to be in touch with and distinguish how we feel about a child, a person or a situation.
- Recognition of how emotional responses enable us to interact construc-tively with others can be beneficial for children and families with whom we work.
- It is acceptable to acknowledge our own emotional vulnerabilities whilst maintaining a professional stance.
- Learning to process our feelings about things that are out of our control must be practiced. When we are unable to influence change or an out-come for a child, it doesn't necessarily mean that we have failed.

Looking after ourselves

Designated safeguarding leads recognise the importance of self-care when undertaking such an important and sometimes difficult role. I asked some safe-guarding leads to tell me about some of the strategies they use to help them with this. One lead a manager in a day-care setting was able to turn to col-leagues within her team to share some the emotional burdens she carried as lead. Another, a childminder, had limitations in relation to collegial support available to them given their work circumstances. Childminders and nannies understandably struggle with this when working independently. One childmin-der, when addressing her concerns about the welfare of a child and having to navigate a poor multi-agency response and engagement, referred to support from her 'extremely supportive family' at a time when she felt 'very isolated'. She found working with other services 'overwhelming' given the lack of infor-mation and support from them towards her efforts to support the child. Looking after our own wellbeing needs is essential if we are to be productive and effective in our lead role. Being able to function as best we can by attending to our own health needs is important. Leads must invest in physical, emotional and mental wellbeing strategies and interventions. otherwise their ability to help others is compromised.

Designated safeguarding leads reflect upon how they address their self-care needs:

Nursery Manager

* Having personal resilience.
* Knowing my own limits.
* Having a supportive partner who could read my moods and emotions.
* Receiving support from others, such as appropriate staff in the setting.
* Having contact with the local authority safeguarding lead.
* Being able to take time out.

Childminder

* Having a supportive family who recognised my emotional needs.
* Being resilient.
* Support from some outside agencies.
* Eating healthy food and getting plenty of sleep.
* Being outdoors and away from the setting.
* Knowing when to step back and take some time away from the issue.

Circle of influence

Recognising and acknowledging our professional limitations can help with self-care. There will be times or situations that are out of our control causing us to feel anxious or powerless. Accepting this position as a safeguarding lead is necessary if we are to put things into some helpful perspective. Turning our nervous energies into those that drive forward what can change or influence not only focusses on the possible, but it helps us manage our own wellbeing.

Stephen Covey's circle of influence model can help safeguarding leads put into some perspective the way we view things that make us most anxious and

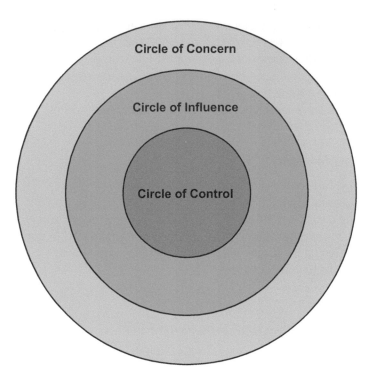

Figure 3.1   Adapted from Covey's circle of concern, influence and control (Stephen
           Covey 1989)

are out of our control alongside the circumstances that we can actively influence to bring about change.

For example:

Circle of concern – We worry about a child who is at risk of emotional
harms because their parent repeatedly enters abusive personal relationships
that involve conflict and domestic abuse. The parent is vulnerable, they have
experienced abuse themselves as a child and they have poor self-esteem. This
situation is out of our control.

Circle of influence – There are some things that we *can* do. We can actively
raise concerns about the child's emotional harms and needs with other agencies so that they can act. We can encourage the child's attendance at nursery
and make sure that they are supported whilst they are in the setting. We can

grasp every possible opportunity to build a relationship with the child's parent to build their self-esteem and help them develop future resilience, which in turn helps them make better decisions and choices in relationships.

Circle of control – Recognising the things that are within our control offer self-assurances reminding us that our input to the situation is not in vain. When the child is in our care rather than at home or elsewhere, they are in a safe and supportive environment. Skilled and knowledgeable practitioners working with the child can meet their needs. We can monitor the ongoing situation, recognising if a situation changes or escalates. We are competent and confident safeguarding leads who know what to do if a child needs help or protection and will act accordingly.

TIME TO REFLECT

Think of a situation with a child you work with that gives you concern and is out of your control. Note the areas of influence you have as safeguarding lead and things that are in your control that help meet the child's needs.

Looking after others

Being mindful of the big emotions that occur when we engage in safeguarding or child protection, it is essential that leads place specific consideration towards looking after others in their teams. The most powerful and influential tool that any leader possesses is that of **role modelling**. When staff observe the ways in which safeguarding leads respond to the emotional pressures of the job and take care of their own wellbeing, these messages communicate the importance of emotional wellbeing across the whole team. A meaningful and authentic approach to staff wellbeing in this context will involve aspects that are far more outreaching than the staff reward or recognition approaches. Staff may welcome the kind words of gratitude or lovely gestures from leads that make them feel valued and appreciated, but these responses will fall short of addressing the most important elements of their wellbeing. Staff may feel under confident and afraid to engage in safeguarding practices, believing that they may make mistakes or do something wrong. They may experience feelings of helplessness in the light of not being able to help a child in their care. Negative experiences or poor or non-engagement from other professionals could result in them feeling inferior. Their concerns may be dismissed because of their professional status and how this may be perceived as unimportant or being less important than others. They may be emotionally overwhelmed because of witnessing first-hand or hearing about abuse that is happening to a child they care for. Parents who are manipulative or working hard to deceive those who are professionally curious about their child may sidestep safeguarding leads and attempt to draw in less experienced or less senior staff in their efforts to hide dangerous behaviours or demonstrate false compliance. In this instance staff need support to identify what is happening and to respond as part of a wider collective to address the situation. John (2008) draws attention to the fact that 'people who work with complexity, discouragement and distress are at risk of becoming overburdened discouraged and distressed as well'. In other words, the negative elements of child protection can be contagious to those working within it.

When safeguarding leads look after other staff in their setting their approach must be both significant and thorough. This involves **mentoring** and **coaching** approaches that support personal resilience and growth. Team members will benefit from this in lots of ways.

- Having a senior or more experienced person to provide sound leadership and direction that they can follow.
- Inspiring and helping them to succeed and excel in their role.
- Supporting them to develop resilience and strategies that help them to manage their emotions and feelings.
- Imparting knowledge and instilling confidence.
- Showing appreciation and recognising their commitments towards children and families with whom they work.
- Providing personal support tailored to their specific needs that is provided consistently over time.

Facilitating on behalf of other staff in the setting is another important function of the safeguarding lead. Leads can often act to make things happen when others get stuck with a situation or if they are faced with a complicated issue that requires someone more knowledgeable or experienced than them to help move it forward. A lead who recognises when and how to facilitate support for others will empower them to not only achieve an outcome but help them to gain personal confidence and learn new skills as they do so.

In conclusion

To be an effective designated safeguarding lead working in the early years we must achieve a whole range of things. We are required to act and operate within the confines of the law demonstrating our **compliance** towards all that is legally expected of us. From this basis our **competencies** are further extended through sound knowledge and an understanding of safeguarding and child protection that underpins practice. **Confident** leads bring together all that they have acquired to be successful in their role. The three components within this vital position are intrinsically linked, forming the bedrock which leads build upon.

Key messages from chapter three

• Safeguarding knowledge is so much more than a tick box exercise.
• Competent leaders draw upon the unique qualities of character as well as vital skills they acquire to undertake their role effectively.
• Designated safeguarding leads undertake their role by applying various leadership models that are appropriate for the task at hand. They will skilfully adopt strategies that ensure children remain central in their efforts to keep them safe and well.
• Managing the big emotions that come with the role of the safeguarding lead can be extremely difficult and needs careful consideration.
• Self-care and staff wellbeing is an important feature for practitioners working to safeguard and protect children.

References

Covey, S. (1989). *The Seven Habits of Highly Effective People*. London: Simon and Shuster UK.

Department for Education. (2021). *The Statutory Framework for the Early Years Foundation Stage: Setting the Standards for Learning, Development and Care for Children from Birth to Five*. Department for Education.

Goleman, D. (1996). *Emotional Intelligence: Why It Can Matter More Than IQ*. London: Bloomsbury Paperbacks.

Harris, A. (2002). *Leadership Concepts and Analytical Tools*. Cited in National Professional Qualification of Integrated Centre Leadership – National College for School Leadership (2008).

HM Gov. (2018). *Working Together to Safeguard Children. A Guide to Inter-agency Working to Safeguard and Promote the Welfare of Children*. HM Gov.

John, K. (2008). Sustaining the Leaders of Children's Centres: The Role of Leadership Mentoring. *European Early Education Research Journal*. 56.

Llywodraeth Cymru Welsh Government. (2022). *Working Together to Safeguard People: Code of Safeguarding Practice*. Llywodraeth Cymru Welsh Government.

National Society for the Prevention of Cruelty to Children. (2021). *Early Years Sector: Learning from Case Reviews*. Summary of Key Issues and Learning for Improved Practice in the Early Years Sector.

Ryan, M. (1999). *The Children Act 1989. Putting It into Practice*. Second Edition. Ashgate.

Siraj-Blatchford, I., and Hallet, E. (2014). *Effective and Caring Leadership in the Early Years*. London: Sage.

Siraj-Blatchford, I., and Manni, L. (2007). *Effective Leadership in the Early Years Sector (The ELEYS Study)*. London: Institute of Education.

The Children Act. (1989). Legilstaion.gov.uk

The Children Act. (2004). Legislation.gov.uk

The Childcare Act. (2006). Legislation.gov.uk

Identifying risk factors in the lives of young children

In previous chapters we have established the extent of vulnerability in very young children and how we recognise different types of abuse that they may be presented with. We have also begun to consider effective strategies that early years practitioners can apply and engage with to help and protect children with whom they work.

This chapter continues to emphasise the **identify** component and focusses on specific risk factors that present to children and how they manifest through child abuse and neglect. We will look at some key themes to support practitioners' knowledge with focus on some relevant subjects relating to their impact upon young children.

Recognised risks for young children

Risks for babies and young children are known to be predominantly found in the home. Many risks at home include common and repetitive themes.

The toxic trio

Recognised risk factors for children often include exposure to *domestic abuse, parental substance abuse* (drugs and/or alcohol) and *parental poor mental health*. These single factors alone threaten children's safety and wellbeing but when they come together, as they often do, they have catastrophic consequences for children. The three commonly identified

DOI: 10.4324/9781003137054-4

features or vulnerabilities that present in parents' lives are referred to as the *toxic trio*. Numerous case reviews feature the toxic trio as contributing towards known risks to children. For countless children who are subjects of case reviews it is too late to change the trajectory or outcome. Practitioners should always be alert and vigilant when working with children from families where the toxic trio is known, taking swift and appropriate actions to address children's safety as a matter of urgency.

Poverty, disadvantage and its impact upon children

As previously noted, poverty is not an indicator suggesting that children will experience abuse or neglect, however it is well documented that low economic status which underpins poverty has significant correlation with poor outcomes for children and is therefore intrinsically associated with vulnerability and disadvantage. Children experiencing poverty, especially in their early years, will be less likely to develop cognitive or social and emotional skills. Their health outcomes are often compromised leading to poor diet and malnutrition. Childhood obesity and poor dental health remains one of the most significant concerns for children living in poverty. Data and analysis from the Little Village Family Poverty Report (2022) in collaboration with Joseph Roundtree Foundation noted that 'child poverty rates remain high for families with a child aged under five years old'. The most concerning data reveals that '1.3 million of the 4.2 million children in poverty in the UK are babies and children under the age of five'. It is predicted that this figure will rise to 5.2 million children by 2023/2024.

Noteworthy features that go hand in hand with poverty:

- Infant mortality.
- Low birth rate in babies.
- Illness and disease, especially respiratory illnesses due to poor living conditions or a child living with an adult who is a smoker.
- Accidents in the home.
- Unintentional injuries.
- Eviction and homelessness.
- Financial difficulties and debt.
- Poor access to services.
- Acute anxiety and stress in the home.

- Adult mental health concerns.
- Poor speech and language.
- Children's readiness to learn is compromised and their educational achievements are poor.
- Antisocial behaviours and school exclusion.
- Employment and economic sustainability in adulthood is hindered due to childhood poverty.

Poverty can lead to family breakdown, conflict and crisis. This in turn can lead to incidents of domestic abuse and involvement in petty crime and criminality.

The COVID-19 pandemic highlighted tremendous effects upon families already experiencing disadvantage and led to others experiencing first-hand the challenges that poverty and disadvantage can bring. Going forward both within the current challenging economic climate and moving towards a cost-of-living crisis in the UK, poverty continues to threaten young children's life outcomes and wellbeing.

Injuries in non-mobile children – learning from a serious case review

In chapter one we identified babies under 12 months in particular as being disproportionately represented in case reviews. We also considered the importance of recognising a heightened level of concern for non-mobile children who receive injuries and bruising when they are not yet moving. I want to take some time to re-visit this theme taking a further look at the risks for non-mobile children. I will be referring to the learning taken from a serious case review into Baby F. This 11-week-old baby was known to a nursery who were caring for him at the time that he sustained serious injury as result of physical abuse perpetrated by the baby's father.

Please be aware that the following details might be hard for some to read.

Summary of events

Baby F was 11 weeks old when he suffered a life-changing head injury. He was of African/European heritage. Both parents in their early and late twenties were receiving support from health professionals due to recognised poor mental health. The mother and father of Baby F had both been diagnosed with post-natal depression. In 2016 Baby F was rushed to hospital as an emergency due to life threatening head injuries. These injuries presented in the form of a swelling on the brain. A medical examination revealed that he had an 'intercranial haemorrhage (bleeding to the brain) and a number of rib fractures and a healing rib fracture'. Both parents were arrested and charged in relation to his injuries. Agencies with recognised involvement for Baby F included:

- A general practitioner (GP).
- Hospital staff.
- Midwife.
- Health visitor.
- Nursery.
- Counselling services prescribed by the GP for both parents.

The review detailed that both parents 'struggled with the demands of a new baby'. The health visitor noted that Baby F's mother reported to them a number of significant factors that alerted concerns and indicated that she was under great pressure. The contributing factors that made things all the more challenging for Baby F were listed in the review.

- The pregnancy was unplanned.
- Mother presented as having 'low mood'.
- There were tensions in the parents' relationship.
- Mother had difficulties with sleeping.
- She was anxious about bonding with the baby.
- There were problems with breast feeding.
- Mother was not waking for the baby at night.
- There was a lack of family support.

There was more than one occasion where Baby F was taken to hospital with concerning symptoms initially not acted upon. There were clear indicators that he was at risk from injury from his father, who had told a GP that he had thoughts of 'harming his baby'. When Baby F was four weeks old, he was offered a place at a nursery. Specific records of his attendance at the nursery are not stated in the review but we do know that he attended when he was eight weeks old, which coincided with a disclosure from his father to a health visitor that he was struggling with his mental health.

A missed opportunity

The review reported that just days before Baby F presented at hospital with a serious head injury he had been 'observed by nursery staff to have a small mark on his cheek which may or may not have been a bruise'. When asked about this as part of the review, staff described the bruise as being 1 x 1.2 cm showing discoloration of the baby's skin. Due to the colour of the baby's skin, staff found it hard to 'decide if this was a bruise or a skin pigmentation'. The review explains that 'staff who were looking after Baby F discussed the mark but reached no decision and no action was taken'.

Having been in many situations where concerning injuries are identified and subsequent discussions take place, I can only speculate what contributed to these discussions for the staff looking after Baby F.

Maybe they talked about their uncertainty in identifying the mark as an injury? I expect that this was the main point of discussion.

Maybe they were worried about making a wrong judgement and taking action that would begin a process that once started would become out of their control?

Maybe they reflected upon their knowledge of or relationship with Baby F's parents, which could have influenced their decision to not take their concerns any further? They could have been over optimistic about what they saw or knew about the parents' relationship between them and their baby. Maybe they were worried about making accusations or suggesting the unthinkable about the parents' actions towards their baby?

We really don't know the context of their discussions, but the review makes it clear that they did not report their concerns to their safeguarding lead which would have potentially been the first step towards following a non-mobile injury protocol of reporting that was in place within their local authority. Polices and protocols such as those initiated by local authority safeguarding partners take away the uncertainty or worry about making independent decisions out of the hands of concerned practitioners. This can only be seen a positive.

In response to the findings of serious case review, the nursery did undertake its own internal review reinforcing the need to follow Local Safeguarding

Partner policies and protocols for bruising and injuries to children who are non-mobile. The nursery also reviewed their recording procedures to make sure that all pre-existing birthmarks were noted for children attending their setting. There are two key points to draw upon from this review: first, the need to recognise and understand risk and, second, always act when risks are known and follow procedures that safeguard and protect children.

Hidden or unseen men – significant others

Referring once more to learning from case reviews, the theme of hidden men occurs frequently, especially in reviews that relate to young children. Hidden men is a phrase used to describe males or significant others in the lives of mothers that are often not taken into account when both identifying risks to children and/or excluded engaging with men (usually fathers) who have potential to provide protective factors for their children. Case reviews capture two main features.

- Men who posed a risk to the child, which resulted in them suffering significant harm.
- Men, for example, estranged fathers who could protect and nurture the child but were overlooked by professionals.

Whilst not stereotyping or assigning a gender-based focus on this theme, the issues relating to known and sometimes unknown dangerous adults having access to children is historically recognised. It is important to refer to the tragedy of Star Hobson who at aged 16 months was murdered by her mother's female partner. Understanding the risks that occur from close relationships between children or significant others, such as adults who have a close relationship with a child's mother and often co-habit or are frequent visitors to the family home, is important for early years practitioners. Working closely with children and families, they will more likely be aware of changes in circumstances including new relationships and/or re-instated relationships that are concerning. For example:

- A child talks about someone new in the family home which raises concerns, or they talk about spending time with someone who is not meant to have contact with them due to previously known risks.

- The mother of a child is seen with someone known to be unsuitable or behave irresponsibly around children. They may be known in the local community or to the police as being dangerous.
- Children are collected from nursery by adults who do not have parental responsibility and expect to take the child regardless because of their relationship status to the child's parent.

A reminder again that in the early years consistent and developing relationships with parents puts practitioners in a strong position to recognise worrying changes or behaviours that impact negatively upon children.

Risk factors relating to 'hidden or unseen men' that have been acknowledged in case reviews:

- Lack of information sharing between adults' and children's services.
- Relying too much on mothers for essential information.
- Not wishing to appear judgemental about parents' personal relationships.
- Overlooking the ability of estranged fathers to provide safe care for their children.

TIME TO REFLECT

What are the most prevalent risk factors identified for children with whom you work or have worked with? How have you identified these risks and what did you do as a result?

Some relevant safeguarding and child protection themes, what they are and how they present risks to young children

The following themes represent a number of topics that are recognised as presenting risks for young children and their families. We will look at each theme and consider the impact that they have upon children. They are by no means the only themes that early years practitioners should be aware of, but feature what I believe to be most relevant and specific currently in relation to child protection practice in the early years.

What is female genital mutilation?

The World Health Organisation defines female genital mutilation (FGM) as comprising 'all procedures that involve partial or total removal of the external female genitalia, or other injury to the female genital organs for non-medical reasons'. There are four major types of mutilation which include:

- Type 1 (clitoridectomy) – removing part or all of the clitoris.
- Type 2 (excision) – removing part or all of the clitoris and cutting the inner and/or outer labia.
- Type 3 (infibulation) – narrowing the vaginal opening.
- Type 4 – other harmful procedures to the female genitals including pricking, piercing, cutting, scraping or burning.

FGM is sometimes known as or referred to as 'cutting' or 'female circumcision'. This act of mutilation that is perpetrated against females can occur when they are first born, during childhood or adolescence, just before marriage or during pregnancy.

FGM was made illegal in the UK under The Prohibition of Female Circumcision Act (1985). Further legislation under the Female Genital Mutilation Act (2003) made it illegal to undertake FGM abroad. Mandatory reporting duties were introduced for teachers through the introduction of the Serious Crime Act (2015). The first conviction in the UK was in February 2019 when a 37-year-old Ugandan woman and her partner were found guilty of performing FGM on their three-year-old daughter.

How might this impact upon young children?

Whatever age a female undergoes FGM, the physical and emotional trauma for them is both significant and harmful. Many practices in the UK and abroad where the procedure is not considered illegal involve crude and barbaric acts upon a child. These procedures are often undertaken by non-medical professionals and with the use of instruments that are that unhygienic and dangerous.

Things to look out for in early years settings that might indicate a girl is at risk of or has undergone FGM

- Knowledge of families, cultures and beliefs.
- Children absent from the setting.
- Observations of injury or infection.
- Unusual behaviour from the child.
- Being aware of conversations, a long holiday abroad or going 'home' to visit a family relative or cutter visiting from abroad, or where only female children are going on holiday.
- A special occasion or ceremony to 'become a woman' or get ready for marriage.
- A female relative being cut – a sister, cousin or an older female relative such as a mother or aunt.

It is expected that all working with children will respond to FGM appropriately. The Early Years Foundation Stage framework (2019) requires staff in early years settings to respond to abuse including abuse 'outside the setting, for example in the child's home or that a girl may have been subjected to (or is at risk of) female genital mutilation'.

Knowledge of a child or concerns of a child who is at risk of or known to have experienced FGM should be made to the police immediately.

What is domestic abuse/violence?

Various legislative contexts define domestic abuse and detail the consequences when domestic abuse is committed. In April 2021 the Domestic Abuse Act became law in England and Wales. This Act created a statutory definition to be used and applied consistently when recognising what constitutes as being abusive behaviour and how to respond to it. *'Domestic abuse is not limited to physical acts of violence or threatening behaviour, and can include emotional, psychological, controlling, or coercive behaviour, sexual and/or economic abuse'* (HM Government 2018). A welcome development reflected within this Act is the recognition that a child who 'sees or hears, or experiences the effects of domestic abuse and is related to the person being abused or the perpetrator is regarded as a victim of domestic abuse' (Gov.UK).

How might this impact upon young children?

Domestic abuse is the most featured characteristic or factor identified when children undergo assessment and are recognised as a child in need; this is when statutory services become concerned about a child's wellbeing or safety. Domestic abuse remains one of the most prevalent and enduring types of abuse that impacts severely upon a child. The impact upon children because of them seeing or hearing domestic abuse is substantial. Furthermore, domestic violence opens up serious harm and emotional trauma for children especially young children. Often adult abusers do not appreciate the direct impact by exposing them to 'volatile situations, which can lead to emotional abuse and their classification as being at risk of significant harm' (Lumsden 2018).

Young children including babies are at risk of abuse if they hear or see domestic abuse between people who are 'personally connected'; this includes parents and family members. Reports of domestic abuse involving children, often young people, upon parent have increased considerably over time.

Children exposed to domestic abuse:

- may be traumatised and unable to regulate their emotions.
- experience anxiety and worry about parents who are victims of domestic abuse when they are away from them whilst at nursery or school.
- display hypervigilance in reading body language or changes in mood or atmosphere.
- become tired or sleepy during the daytime (children who live in homes where domestic abuse occurs find it hard to fall asleep and stay asleep).
- may display aggression towards others.
- become withdrawn.

- seek attention.
- show regression in their development or behaviour.
- have problems controlling their bladders and experience soiling (bed wetting etc.).

What is child criminal exploitation and County Lines?

Child criminal exploitation (CCE) does not have a legal definition, however it has and continues to become a substantial child protection concern and contributes to being a major factor that sits within crimes committed in communities. It involves vulnerable young people and exposes them to serious risks. Inadvertently these risks are most likely to impact upon other family members including younger siblings. Often within the context of CCE, networks known as County Lines play a significant part in these sinister and dangerous activities.

The UK Home Office (2018) describe County Lines to 'describe gangs and organised criminal networks involved in exporting illegal drugs into one or more importing areas within the UK, using dedicated mobile phone lines or other form of "deal line". They are likely to exploit children and vulnerable adults to move and store the drugs and money and they will often use coercion, intimidation, violence (including sexual violence) and weapons'. Children and families who are drawn into County Line activity and are associated with crime relating to the exploitation of children and vulnerable adults are often trapped in positions whereas a result of their vulnerabilities they are exploited and forced or enticed into engaging in criminal activity and exposed to serious abuse with life-threatening consequences.

How might this impact upon young children?

The Children's Commissioner for England (2019) published a report on the extent and impact upon children known to or involved in criminal gangs. Using British Crime Survey data available from the Office of National Statistics, its findings were most concerning. In addition to the large numbers of children being groomed by gangs, identifying as being part of a gang, and knowing and being a victim of gang violence, there were 313,000 children who were recognised as being siblings of gang members. I image that this data will have increased given the prevalence of gang crime over the past years.

Signs that may suggest association with CCE and County Lines in the early years.

- Knowledge of family associations with crime and criminality.
- Children who appear afraid or present with significant changes in behaviour.
- Knowledge of family debt or significant changes in economic circumstances.
- Family members suddenly acquire unusual amounts of wealth or money or high value items.
- Items such as weapons or drugs hidden in children's belongings.
- Talk of violence or violent behaviour displayed.
- Family drug use or evidence of drug use in the child's home.

What is fabricated and induced illness? (FII)

The term 'Fabricated or Induced Illness' was introduced in the UK by the Royal College of Paediatricians and Child Health in 2001. This form of child abuse was also previously known as Munchausen's by Proxy, first officially named in 1977. Fabricated or induced illness normally falls under the category of physical abuse. The abuser may have a history of neglect or drug and alcohol abuse themselves or evidence of a personality disorder which can cause irrational thoughts, disturbed thinking and resentment of their own child. FII can also be a result of financial greed and benefit fraud where the parent or carer gains financial rewards for needing to care for an unwell or disabled child. Whilst FII is quite a rare occurrence, it is important that early years practitioners have knowledge of it especially when caring for young children who are unable to speak out themselves or understand what is happening to them.

Definitions of fabricated or induced illness

FII occurs when a parent or carer, usually the child's biological mother, 'exaggerates or deliberately causes symptoms of illness in a child' (NHS 2019).

'Physical harm may also be caused when a parent or carer fabricates the symptoms of, or deliberately induces, illness in a child' (HM Government 2015).

It is also considered physical abuse if a parent or carer makes up or causes the symptoms of illness in children. For example, they may give them medicine they don't need, making them unwell. This is known as fabricated or induced illness (FII). It is important to remember that physical abuse is any way of intentionally causing physical harm to a child or young person. It also includes making up the symptoms of an illness or causing a child to become unwell (NSPCC 2019).

How might this impact upon young children?

Fabricated or Induced Illness can have several warning signs and can range from severe neglect to parents or carers making the child physically or emotionally unwell. Healthcare professionals can often be persuaded, by the parent or carer, into believing that the child is suffering from a serious illness although they may appear very healthy.

- The child may have frequent or unexplained absences from nursery and school.
- They may have regular appointments at the doctor's or hospital whilst their physical condition at your setting does not give you any cause for concern.
- The parent or carer may make repeated claims that the child is unwell, and they require medical assistance whilst in your care for symptoms that are vague and inconsistent e.g. tummy aches, headaches, dizzy spells, rashes and bowel problems.
- The parent or carer may give confusing or inconsistent stories about physical symptoms.
- There may also be frequent requests for medication to be administered which may or may not be prescribed.
- The parent or carer may become angry and argumentative if challenged regarding the child's condition or need for medication.

TIME TO THINK

How do your safeguarding/child protection and administering of medication policies and procedures support effective practice in regard to recognising and acting upon fabricated and induced illness?

What is child abuse linked to faith or belief? (CALFB)

*Some disturbing content might be difficult to read.

There are a number of definitions or explanations of what child abused linked to faith or belief actually means or refers to. This theme, recognised in the abuse and subsequent deaths of children such as Victoria Climbie (2000) and Khrya Isaq (2008), has seen recent increased attention and discussion in the early years. We also know that there has been a rise in numbers of children known to have experienced abuse that is linked to faith or belief. Gov. UK figures (2021) show around 1,950 suspected child victims of CALFB were identified by English councils in 2018/2019, which is a 34% increase on the previous year.

This definition by the Metropolitan police is succinct and helpful: 'Abuse linked to faith or belief is where concerns for a child's welfare have been identified, and could be caused by, a belief in witchcraft, spirit or demonic possession, ritual or satanic abuse features; or when practices linked to faith or belief are harmful to a child'.

The National FGM Centre who help raise awareness and support victims of CALFB also suggest the following definitions.

* Witchcraft and spirit possession demons or the devil acting through children or leading them astray (traditionally seen in some Christian beliefs).
* The evil eye or djinns (traditionally known in some Islamic faith and contexts) and dakini (in the Hindu context).
* Ritual or muti murders where the killing of children is believed to have supernatural benefits, or the use of their body parts is believed to produce potent magical remedies.
* Use of belief in magic or witchcraft to create fear in children to make them more compliant when they are being trafficked for domestic slavery or sexual exploitation.

Faith groups and the belief in evil spirits

Many religions and faith groups acknowledge a belief in spirits, with some recognising both good and evil features of these spirits. Some within the Christian church believe in spirit procession and make a distinction between the Holy Spirit and evil spirits. Islam also recognises the existence of evil spirits. Some traditional African beliefs lead some to believe that people and children can be taken over by evil spirits.

How might this impact upon young children?

Physical abuse can be displayed by beating the evil spirit out of the child with use of objects and heavy instruments. It can include kicking, punching, burning, cutting and other forms of physical assault. Fasting can also be imposed upon a child leading to starvation.

Emotional abuse underpins the many elements of abuse recognised as a result of witchcraft labelling. Ostracising a child, blaming them for adverse situations, isolating them from others, making them believe that they are evil and have done wrong are just some examples of the emotional effects upon a child.

Neglect in the form of starvation, depriving a child of food, withholding medical attention, and refusing to meet the emotional and psychological needs of a child all constitute abuse in this category. A child who is denied educational opportunities by removing them from school and not providing them with another means of education is also deemed as neglect.

Sexual abuse may occur as a child is isolated from others within the family, removing elements of protective factors that otherwise would be available to them. The more de-valued the child becomes in the context of family and community the more vulnerable they are to sexual abuse.

Some signs that may suggest a child is experiencing witchcraft-related abuse:

- Unexplained bruises or marks on the body including incisions or burns.
- Child believes that they are bad and will go to hell.
- They are ostracised by family, members of the community or faith group to which they belong.
- Irregular or non- attendance at school.
- Tells others that they are fasting.
- Is malnourished or scavenges for food.
- Deterioration in the child's wellbeing.
- Non-attendance to medical needs or not taken to hospital when ill or injured.

Children may experience neglect because parents withhold medical care or attention in the belief that spiritual interventions will cure or heal them rather than medicine or by seeking help from doctors or medical practitioners.

What are online risks and harms?

Risks and dangers for children online continue to gather momentum. With most if not all children including young children spending time online in one way or another, online risks persist and have become even more alarming. The Office for Communications (Ofcom) who regulates the UK communications industry state that 'nearly all children went online in 2021, with the majority using a mobile phone or tablet to do so' (2022). Their report also ascertained that out of those surveyed 89% of three- to four-year-olds use video sharing platforms, which includes 'watching, posting and sharing content on any video sharing platform'. Online risks and harms include a wide range of considerations that are hazardous for children. Uk.Gov guidance (2019) notes three main areas of concern.

1 **Content** – what children see.
   - Exposure to inappropriate videos, pictures or messages which might upset, worry, or frighten them.
   - Intimidating harmful or inappropriate behaviour they see online.
   - Searching for inappropriate content on purpose or stumbling upon it by accident.
   - Inadvertently giving apps or websites permission to share their location or other personal information.
   - Spending real money via in-app or in-games purchases.
2 **Contact** – who might communicate with them.
   - Being abused online (including sexually) by people they don't know, such as when gaming or using video chat.
   - Being abused online (including sexually) by people they know, such as friends and family members.
   - Sending images or information to people on the device's contacts.
3 **Conduct** – how they (children) might behave.
   - Exhibiting unhealthy behaviours and boundaries around use of screens.
   - Being unkind to each other online as well as offline, using mean words or excluding others from their games.

- Using words or terminology which are not appropriate for their age.
- Engaging in unhealthy relationships.
- Taking inappropriate or indecent images and videos of themselves.

How might this impact upon young children?

Online abuse includes:

- Encouraging self-harm or abusive behaviours in a child.
- Sexual abuse including grooming a child in preparation for abuse.
- Exposing children to emotionally harmful content including extremist materials and content.
- Emotionally abusing children including online bullying and intimidation.

TIME TO THINK

How does your setting manage and implement safe online practices for children?

How do you help children stay safe when online?

How do you support parents to help keep their children safe online?

TEAM TALK

Identify where in your early years environment online risks and harms may occur. What online devices do you use in your settings and how do you ensure they are safe for children? When did you last talk to children about online safety and what did this involve and achieve?

Contextual safeguarding and extra-familial threats

The term contextual safeguarding and its approach towards child protection were developed by Dr Carlene Firman. Her research, which challenges many concepts previously considered and applied to child protection responses and systems, is helping practitioners to understand the meaning and risks of 'extra-familial' threats that present to children. Firman defines contextual safeguarding as 'an approach to understanding, and responding to, young people's experiences of significant harm beyond their families'. It recognises that the 'different relationships that young people form in their neighbourhoods, schools and online can feature violence and abuse. Parents and carers have little influence over these contexts, and young people's experiences of extra-familial abuse can undermine parent-child relationships'.

Whilst this explanation of contextual safeguarding references 'young people', we need to remember that these issues will impact upon wider family members also. Young children are also directly at risk of extra-familial harms. Government guidance for England (HM Government 2018) refers to Assessment of risk from outside the home, recognising that children are 'vulnerable to abuse or exploitation from outside their families'. Extra-familial threats for younger children include wider environmental factors such as:

- Threats that arise from school or other places where children receive education.
- Within their peer groups.
- The wider community.
- Online.

These kinds of risks are often more concerning when parents or carers of children are unable to provide appropriate protective factors because they are unaware of the risks, they are hidden from them, or they are unable to intervene to stop them from happening.

TIME TO THINK

Think about the children in your setting. What kind or risks might they be exposed to which are extra-familial, in other words outside of their families influence and protection? What do you know about a child's circumstances or wider family network relationships and the community where they live which may threaten or compromise their safety?

Adverse childhood experiences (ACEs)

There has over recent years been a significant focus and emphasis placed upon adverse childhood experiences, what they refer to and what this means for children who are exposed to them. Research into ACEs has furthered a better understanding of the impact they have upon young children both during childhood and in later life.

Children

I wish that I had known about brain development and neuroscience earlier in my career; ideally this would have been when I worked directly with children, whilst making professional judgements and decisions that impacted upon their wellbeing and safety. Knowing that rapid brain development takes place pre-birth to five and understanding how the architecture of brain development works would have changed the way I worked. I would have known about cortisol, the toxic stress and stress responses that transpire because of child abuse or neglect. This would have helped me to understand a child's lived experience so much better, increasing my ability to see things from their perspective. I would have understood why it was impossible for some children to respond to any encouragement of calm or reason when trauma was present and likely to repeat time and time again. When experiences of neglect had built the expectation of poor or no response from a caring nurturing adult, I would understand better why children struggled to engage or even communicate with someone giving them attention. Understanding how brains are built, the importance of neuron and synapses connection, and the effects of abuse and neglect upon a young developing brain is essential to be a successful and effective safeguarding practitioner in the early years. Conkbayir (2021) describes adverse childhood experiences as 'traumatic events that are uncontrollable to the child, occurring from in utero, which are proven to have pervasive effects on holistic health and wellbeing across the life trajectory'.

Dr Mine Conkbayir – a writer, researcher, and expert in the field of neuroscience – also has extensive experience of working in the early years. Her work and research support those working with children to develop neuroscience informed practices across a wide range of areas such as self and co-regulation and the importance of trauma informed practice. I asked Mine some questions about ACEs and the impact they have upon brain development in young children.

An interview with Dr Mine Conkbayir

Q. Mine, through your work and research you are helping to raise awareness of neuroscience and knowledge of brain development in young children. I'm particularly interested in understanding how poor or abusive experiences impact upon children. How do adverse childhood experiences (ACEs) shape brain development and emotional responses in childhood?
　Mine Conkbayir:

If gone unsupported – and in a timely manner, a child who has been subjected to ACE's, will suffer in terms of their health and wellbeing, not only in the short-term but throughout adulthood too.

Q. How might this manifest?
　Mine Conkbayir:

Well, if a child's brain and body are signalling to her that she is in danger (where in fact, there is no actual sign of danger), her physiology and cognitive abilities will be immediately compromised, as her brain and body will have entered flight or fight mode. So, 'unnecessary' functions like thinking before she acts, controlling her social behaviour and concentrating on her learning will be diminished. This is because the brain and body of a child who has been subjected to ACEs is wired for stress. In line with this, survivors of ACEs tend to have higher baseline cortisol levels which results in hyper-arousal. Over time, continued elevated cortisol levels can weaken the activity of the immune system, resulting in persistent ill health. Broadly speaking, a survivor of ACEs will mainly operate from their downstairs brain (this is the more primitive and emotionally reactive part of the brain), as opposed to their upstairs brain (responsible for all those skills we bunch together under the term 'school readiness' – a term I dislike!). Executive functions like delaying gratification, choosing what to focus on and what to ignore, problem-solving, learning and managing 'big' emotions like fear and anger reside in the upstairs brain.

Q. What does a developing brain need?
   Mine Conkbayir:

It will seem deceptively simply but here are just a few neuroprotective factors needed to ensure healthy building and strengthening of synaptic connectivity in those important early years:

- Healthy pregnancy.
- Secure attachment.
- Absence of toxic stress.
- Abundant social interaction.
- Co-regulation.
- High-quality pre-school provision.
- Stimulating experiences.
- Regular physical activity.
- Optimum nutrition.

Upon reading this non-exhaustive list, ask yourself, do you know the attachment history of the children with whom you work? How was mum's pregnancy? Was she depressed? Did she have support? Is home a safe place?

Q. What de-rails healthy brain development in young children?
   Mine Conkbayir:

I think we need to acknowledge the short- and long-term impact of ACEs, these being:

- Abuse (sexual, emotional and physical).
- Neglect.
- Dysfunctional home environment.
- Domestic abuse (or domestic violence).
- Parental mental health issues.
- Parental substance misuse.
- Parental separation/divorce.
- Parental imprisonment.

Think of all you had or did not have access to emotionally, as a child. A child who is devoid of nurturing and responsive relationships may develop a perception of a world that is cold and uncaring. They will also find it difficult to self-regulate their emotional responses to the trials and tribulations of life, struggling with school and later – work and relationships. Where children do not have a safe and nurturing experience, I believe it is our responsibility to help nurture their self-regulation and their unique ability to thrive.

Q. How important is the quality of early care for children who have experienced trauma?
    Mine Conkbayir:

In my opinion, it is life-saving. Nurseries and schools are a haven, a sanctuary for children who live in chaotic or abusive homes. The adults, their key persons and the experiences provided in that setting can go a long way in supporting the child to self-regulate their emotional responses, to build a positive self-image and social skills through the relationships and activities and relationships provided. But – this requires an understanding of early brain development and the neuroscience of ACEs. Until this is provided as standard across early years qualifications and training, I fear that we will miss this opportunity to reach the thousands of children who are survivors of ACEs – because the current priority is testing and labelling of children, and this must stop.

Adults

Adverse childhood experiences frequently thematically feature in numerous safeguarding case reviews acknowledging the detrimental effects of adverse childhood experiences upon parents of children who have been abused or neglected. This in no way draws conclusions or assumptions about intergenerational abuse and the certainty about ongoing abuse – for example if a child experiences abuse, they will them go on to abuse themselves. It does however tell us that for some adults their ability to provide protective factors for their children can be severely compromised because of their own adverse experiences. The Early Intervention Foundation (2018) reported the strong association between the 'number of ACE's and the risks of mental health problems, involvement in crime and other poor outcomes in later life'. We will refer to this again when considering working with parents in chapter 6.

TIME TO REFLECT

How can you increase your knowledge of neuroscience and ACEs in order to help you better identify children's lived experiences?

How might understanding ACEs impact upon your practice when supporting children who experience abuse and neglect?

Children with additional vulnerabilities

Additional vulnerabilities for children who have **special educational needs** or those determined as being **neurodivergent** should be taken into account when recognising risk factors. Children who have **physical disabilities** and those with limited or no communication remain most vulnerable. Children who identify as neurodivergent such as children with attention deficit hyperactivity disorder (ADHD), autism, or Tourette's syndrome may experience abuse because their behaviours or unique traits are misunderstood by others. This may lead to peers and adults responding to them in ways that are harmful to their wellbeing and in some circumstances their safety. Vulnerabilities extend to children from marginalised groups or those who may experience adverse responses from others in the form of racism and discrimination.

TIME TO REFLECT

Think about children in your setting and what makes them vulnerable. What strategies do you have in place to support them and keep them safe?

Figure 4.1   It makes me happy when I go to the beach.

Key messages from chapter four

* Some risks for young children are more prevalent than others.
* Circumstances in the lives of parents/carers such as poor mental health, substance abuse and domestic abuse significantly impacts negatively upon children.
* Early years practitioners need to be aware of safeguarding themes that highlight risks to children they work with.
* It is important to understand the risks to children within the family context whilst being aware that some risks will occur from outside of the family also.
* Adverse experiences are extremely harmful both in early childhood and beyond.
* Early years practitioners should understand the impact of ACEs upon young children's healthy brain development.
* Disability, difference and prejudice makes children more vulnerable to abuse.

References

Baby, F., and Tudor, K. (2020). Plymouth Safeguarding Children Board. *Serious Case Review.* 22.

Children and Parents: Media Use and Attitudes Report 2022. (2022). Ofcom.

Children's Commissioner. (2019). *Keeping Kids Safe: Improving Safeguarding Responses to Gang Violence and Criminal Exploitation.* Children's Commissioner.

Conkbayir, M. (2021). *Early Childhood and Neuroscience. Theory, Research and Implications for Practice.* Second Edition. London and New York: Bloomsbury.

Contextual Safeguarding. *Our History – Contextual Safeguarding Network.* (https://safeguarding.network/content/contextual-safeguarding/#:~:text=Contextual%20safeguarding%20identifies%20that%20no%20child%20or%20young,and%20young%20people%20that%20we%20understand%20these%20influences.)

Criminal Exploitation of Children and Vulnerable Adults: County Lines Guidance. (2018). Home Office.

Department for Education. (2021). *The Statutory Framework for the Early Years Foundation Stage: Setting the Standards for Learning, Development and Care for Children from Birth to Five*. Department for Education.

The Early Intervention Foundation. (2018). *Realising the Potential of Early Intervention*. The Early Intervention Foundation.

Gov.UK. (2019). *Safeguarding Children and Protecting Professionals in Early Years Settings*. Online Considerations. Gov.UK.

Gov.UK. (2021). *Characteristics of Children in need Reporting Year 2021*. Explore Education Statistics (explore-education-statistics.service.gov. uk).

HM Gov. (2015). *What to Do If You're Worried about a Child Being Abused. Advice for Practitioners*. HM Gov.

HM Gov. (2018). *Working Together to Safeguard Children. A Guide to Inter-agency Working to Safeguard and Promote the Welfare of Children*. HM Gov.

Lumsden, E. (2018). *Child Protection in the Early Years. A Practical Guide*. London: Jessica Kingsley Publishers.

Metropolitan Police. *Child abuse Linked to Faith or Belief*. Metropolitan Police (https://www.met.police.uk/advice/advice-and-information/caa/child-abuse/faith-based-abuse/).

Moreau, S. (2022). *It Takes a Village*. Little Village.

National FGM Centre. *Child Abuse Linked to Faith or Belief*. National FGM Centre.

NHS. (2019). *Overview – Fabricated and Induced Illness*. NHS (www. nhs.uk).

NSPCC. (2019). *What is Child Abuse? What is Child Abuse & How to Keep Your Child Protected*. NSPCC.

Statutory Definition of Domestic Abuse Factsheet. Updated January 2022. Gov.UK (www.gov.uk).

World Health Organisation. (2022). *Female Genital Mutilation* (who.int).

Taking action to safeguard and protect children

Taking action is a crucial element that defines effective safeguarding practice. The incentive to act should a child require help or protection must always be motivated by the child's needs. The processes that follow actions taken can often steer practitioners in other directions leading them away from the child. For example, a parent who avoids being questioned about a situation or who offers excuses for unacceptable behaviours or personal conduct has the potential to delay or prevent action from being taken. The national review (2022) into the death of Arthur Labinjo-Hughes, the six-year-old who was abused and murdered by his father and his partner, makes this point concluding that 'Arthur's voice was often mediated by his father'. It found that assessments made by professionals very much 'relied on the fathers' perspectives and not Arthur's'. Sometimes when colleagues and multi-agency partners don't share the same concerns or sense of urgency, this has the potential to discourage practitioners from pursuing a course of action. Early years practitioners should stand firm and not be deterred from their decision to act if they believe this to be in the best interests of the child.

Considering the components mentioned previously, this chapter features mostly **Help, Protect** and **Report.** We will look at these to differentiate between the levels of needs for children and therefore the different actions or responses that should follow once the child's needs have been established.

What is meant by safeguarding and child protection?

I have intentionally referred to safeguarding and child protection separately because they have different characteristics. Being able to distinguish between both is important. The National Society for the Prevention

DOI: 10.4324/9781003137054-5

of Cruelty to Children (NSPCC) have a helpful definition. It describes safe-guarding as 'the action that is taken to promote the welfare of children and protect them from harm'.

Safeguarding therefore refers to:

* protecting children from abuse and maltreatment.
* preventing harm to children's health or development.
* ensuring children grow up with the provision of safe and effective care.
* taking action to enable all children and young people to have the best outcomes.

The definition recognises **child protection** as 'part of the safeguarding pro-cess', focussing on 'protecting individual children identified as suffering or likely to suffer significant harm'. When considering child protection this also includes 'procedures which detail how to respond to concerns about a child'.

What does it mean to take safeguarding or child protection action?

Taking actions that safeguard and protect children cover a wide range of things from responding to children's prompts or cues both subtle and obvious. Effective safeguarding practitioners will constantly take actions to promote chil-dren's welfare and ensure that they are always safe and well.

TIME TO REFLECT

Think about the safeguarding or child protection processes that involve taking action within the *context of your role*. What do they include?

TEAM TALK

Think about one typical day in your setting, writing down all the things that are done that involve taking action to safeguard or protect children.

When children are introduced to a new early years setting or when practitioners begin to work with them, lots of information is gathered and documented. This involves initial actions that amongst other things will also feature preventative measures to safeguard children. Questions will be asked about the following:

- What are the child's health needs and how do we meet them?
- Who has parental responsibility?
- Who are relevant and significant adults in the life of the child and what is their relationship to the child?
- Are there other agencies working with the child and/or family?
- Has an early help assessment been done for the child (are they receiving early intervention support)? If so, what is stated in the agreed plan for them? Is this plan still active?
- Is the child known to social care, either considered as being a child in need or on a child protection plan (or equivalent, outside of England)? If so, what are the reasons for this and how will early years practitioners working with the child support and engage in the subsequent processes involved?

Other activities that require all practitioners to act:

- Inquisitive actions that look further into a situation or circumstance, requiring practitioners to be professionally curious.
- Validation, checking out facts.
- Investigation, seeking further information or details from parents or other professionals about a child or family.
- Substantiation of information or details shared that ensure accurate knowledge is the basis upon which we determine our response.

Understanding levels of need

Reference to the extent of need or level of need for a child is crucial to acknowledge appropriate responses and actions that should be taken.

In England, Local Safeguarding Partners (LSPs) provide guidance using thresholds or a continuum of need. These are determined by each local authority LSP and are used to recognise and respond to need in keeping with local expectations. I am aware that not all UK countries use thresholds but for those who do, they are an essential tool that guides practitioners especially those with lead safeguarding responsibilities to apply and use in practice.

Each local authority has its unique threshold and much to the frustration of those who work across more than one area they all vary. Some threshold diagrams and approaches are known as windscreen wiper models, symbolising the fluidity or movement of a child's needs which can increase or decrease. Others may present as a pyramid or diagram that demonstrates a continuous movement should a child's needs escalate to that of a higher level or de-escalate to a lower level. Thresholds will emphasise levels where children can be supported by single agencies, through multi-agency involvement and where statutory agencies are required by law to act, intervene and support. Levels vary between 1 and 4 or 1 and 5 depending on each local authority. Behind the colourful summary or diagram will be a more detailed text explaining each level and what examples of need these levels refer to.

Some examples

Level 1 – Universal

A child whose needs are recognised as being at Level 1, often universal level, will be determined as such in that they can and will most likely achieve outcomes with support from universal services. Universal services represent health care, education such as school or early years, leisure services or various services delivered by private, voluntary and independent sectors. To access such services children do not require assessment or referral.

Level 2 – Early help – additional needs

At this lower level of early help (early intervention) the additional identified needs of a child may be met by one single agency such as through early years provision. The child may receive some direct support from practitioners focussing on things such as speech and language, behavioural challenges, family bereavement, difficulties due to changes in economic status or support that takes into consideration emotional and physical disruptions because of homelessness or eviction. Children's needs can be adequately met by single agency support and relevant interventions such as those delivered by early years practitioners. Early help assessments may take place at this level of intervention depending upon the local authority directive.

Level 3 – Early help – complex needs

This higher level of early help will reflect children's needs as being more complex. It often includes multiple needs that will require the coming together of more than one agency that can support the child's needs. A coordinated and targeted approach to meeting the needs of the child will be necessary and determined by the process of early help assessment, which will involve multi-agency input and engagement. A lead professional will be appointed to assist in the coordination of the early help process. A plan will be determined, agreed by the child's parents and others working with the child. Sometimes these processes that take place in England are termed as 'team around the family' or 'team around the child'. As early help is NOT a statutory requirement, consent from the child's parents is necessary for the process to take place.

Level 4 – Child in need (CIN)

Children who are referred to as a 'child in need' will sometimes be represented at Level 4 in thresholds. The term child in need which is defined in section 17 of the Children Act 1989 refers to 'a child who is unlikely to achieve a satisfactory level of health or development, or their health and development will be significantly impaired, without the provision of services; or a child who is disabled'. Specialist support is required at this level of threshold and social care will be part of the child in need process.

Level 5 – Child at risk of significant harm

The highest level of threshold will always refer to children who need protection due to risk of 'significant harm'. Reference to section 47 of the Children Act 1989 is central to this highest level of need. Children's needs therefore reflect that they may be at risk of harm or likely to suffer harm. Statutory interventions are required to take place to protect a child. This includes contacting the police if the child is in immediate danger or social care; it can involve making a referral which if successful will begin processes to protect a child. Assessment at this level of need is undertaken by a social worker, which may in turn lead to the child becoming subject to a child protection plan. Other countries in the UK sometimes refer to this outcome as being on a 'child protection register'.

TIME TO REFLECT

If you work in England, what does your threshold or continuum of need tell you about levels of need for children in your local authority? How many levels are there, and can you identify how they differentiate and determine levels of need for children who need early help and those who need protection?

If you don't work as a practitioner in England, what does your local authority use to determine levels of need for children? How do you use this to inform decisions that lead to taking action for a child?

Help
Early intervention – early help

Background and context

In 2010, child protection expert Professor Eileen Munro was commissioned by the UK Government to produce an independent review into child protection systems in England. The purpose of the review (2011) was to make recommendations and reform child protection systems, shifting the main emphasis from that of compliance to a system that 'keeps a focus on children, checking whether they are being effectively helped, and adapting when problems are identified'. The report concentrated on several themes mostly setting out clear principles that contribute to effective child protection systems, how they feature in practice and most importantly how they impact positively upon children. A whole chapter in the Munro report was dedicated to early help, drawing attention to the need for shared responsibilities for the provision of early help and how this could best be achieved. The report led to lots of discussions and debate about early intervention in general. Whilst the concept was not new, it was fast becoming recognised that targeted efforts and dedicated resources prioritised to deliver early help services for children was both a significant and progressive development. At the time that the report was published, I had been invited to join a new and exciting early intervention service operating in a Greater Manchester local authority. This developing service incorporated the city's children's centres, including local authority day nursery provision, family support teams working with pre-birth to school age children and developed a wide range of services that championed the efforts of intervening early in the lives of children and their families. Both international and national research into the successes and huge advancements that early intervention had made in children's lives is conclusive – it works! Most importantly, research highlights the appropriate ethical approach as its main priority and focus, this being its aim to improve lifelong outcomes for children. Early help also makes economic sense, contributing to reducing costs for struggling local authorities. As a child's needs increase the costs associated with statutory engagement and processes also rise. Addressing needs sooner is a cost-effective model as well as an ethical approach that centres on the child.

There was a call at one time for the Government to make early help a statutory requirement or duty for local authorities, aligning it with that of child in need or child protection status, however this didn't happen. In fact, sadly a significantly de-prioritised emphasis from Government has led to less investment and a reduction in efforts directed at services such as children's centres and targeted youth services over time. The impact of significantly reduced early intervention services for children is evident and most concerning. Action for Children (2022) in their 2022 report concluded data analysed from 2015–2016 to 2019–2020, showing an estimated '1.26 million occasions where a closed assessment (to social care) did not lead to an early help referral' when it should have. In 25% of these cases, the child in question was re-referred to social care within 12 months, suggesting 'early help support might have helped them in the interim'. The overarching headlines in the report showed that '60,000 opportunities to offer early help' occur each year every year. That for 'every two children receiving early help 'there are already three children in social care' and that nine out of ten local authorities cut early intervention spending between 2015–2016 and 2019–2020. This being the period leading up to the COVID-19 pandemic where of course early help services were most needed.

What is early intervention – early help?

The Early Intervention Foundation has a helpful explanation that simplifies the meaning of early intervention.

> Early intervention means identifying and providing early support to children and young people who are at risk of poor outcomes, such as mental health problems, poor academic attainment, or involvement in crime or antisocial behaviour. Effective early intervention works to prevent problems occurring, or to tackle them head-on before they get worse.
>
> (2018).

When we consider the importance of intervening in the lives of our youngest of children, **early help** and the **early years** are intrinsically linked. It is vital therefore that early years safeguarding practices include child-centred strategies that offer early help outcomes for all young children.

Government guidance in England (2018) draws attention to the overarching aims of early help, noting its effectiveness in 'promoting the welfare of children' rather than 'reacting later'. It urges practitioners to provide early help 'as soon as the problem emerges at any time in the life of a child'. It recognises that early help can 'prevent further problems from arising'.

The guidance lists some reasons as to why practitioners should 'be alert to the potential need' for early help if a child or young person;

- Is disabled and has specific additional needs.
- Has special educational needs (whether or not they have a statutory education, health and care plan).

- Is a young carer.
- Is showing signs of engaging in anti-social or criminal behaviour, including gang involvement and association with organised crime groups.
- Is frequently missing/goes missing from care or from home.
- Is misusing drugs or alcohol themselves.
- Is in a family circumstance presenting challenges for the child, such as substance misuse, adult mental health problems and domestic abuse.
- Has returned home to their family from care.
- Is showing early signs of abuse and/or neglect.
- Is at risk of being radicalised.
- Is privately fostered.
- Has a parent/carer in custody.

Taking action to help a child

Once a child's needs have been identified, they require analysis and consideration. As previously stated, children whose needs can be met through early intervention may receive support from one single agency and formal assessment will not be required. If the child's needs are complex or in order to meet their needs a number of professionals are required to support targeted interventions, an **early help assessment** will be done. This includes sharing and drawing upon information as part of a wider group of multi-agency professionals who are working with the child. Representation from this group will vary depending on the reason for the interventions, but often young children will receive multi-agency support from professionals such as health visitors, general practitioners, speech and language specialists or local authority family support workers. A coordinated response and approach to assessment followed by devising an **early help plan** to achieve agreed outcomes for the child is the next essential step. A **lead professional** will be appointed to enable effective and coordinated delivery of the plan that is inclusive of all those involved and very much involving parents' input and contributions. The lead professional and others will manage and monitor progress made. Lack of engagement from parents may become a key feature that requires challenge and, if necessary, scrutiny. When a parent does not engage with early help processes and this becomes detrimental to the child, consideration as to whether the child's needs have or will escalate to a higher level is taken by professionals.

Further considerations

- Early help is not a statutory requirement. This means that local authorities do not have a legal duty to support a child with early help services as they do with children who are child in need or at risk of significant harm as defined in the Children Act 1989.
- Early help assessment requires consent from the child's parent or legal guardian.
- Information sharing plays a vital role in effective early help practice.
- Early help processes often provide clarity when things are not yet clear or uncertain for a child.
- Effective early help assessment and interventions require good partnership working with others including professionals who are experts in their field such as health/medical professionals, schools and early years practitioners.
- A child who has previously been subject to a child protection plan or a child in need and whose levels of needs are de-escalating should receive and benefit from early help support.

Early help in early years

Children in the early years who are supported through early help or interventions and services may be identified as follows.

- A child requiring extra support as identified through summative assessment such as the Progress check age two (Early Years Foundation Stage – England).
- A child with an education, health and care plan (England).
- A child identified as needing early intervention support by their 'named person' (Getting it right for every child – Scotland).

Protect
Significant harm – what is significant harm?

When considering the need to protect a child we refer to a child at risk of significant harm. A reminder that significant harm is the level of threshold by which statutory services have a legal duty to intervene. Physical, sexual, emotional abuse and neglect featured in chapter four define the categories that can amount to significant harm. The Children Act (1989) (Section 31, Children Act 1989; Article 2, Children (Northern Ireland) Order 1995; defines harm as the ill treatment or impairment of health and development. Impairment is also determined in relation to a child witnessing the ill treatment of another for instance in the context of domestic violence.

Moving towards a new concept of Family Help

Recommendations made in The Independent Review of Children's Social Care (2022) include a new and transformative approach in providing services for children and families. The proposal is to introduce 'one category of "Family Help" to replace "targeted early help" and the "child in need" work, providing families with much higher levels of meaningful support'. This perceived revolution will 'be available to any family facing significant challenges that could pose a threat to providing their child with a loving, stable, safe family life'. Family Help services will be delivered by a range of multi-disciplined professionals supporting children who are 'receiving targeted early help' or who are on a child in need or child protection plan. The wider implications of this development stand to address the growing complex needs for children and families and the overwhelming challenges within social care.

Acting in response to abuse and neglect
Responding to a child's disclosure

Understanding why children don't always speak out.

Before considering how children disclose abuse or neglect and our responses should they do so, it is important to first understand why children don't always tell others about their adverse experiences.

* Younger children are of course unable to communicate verbally and for some limited language development will mean that they cannot yet articulate emotions or put into words what they want to tell us. This is where

practitioners need to be super tuned in to the children they know well in order to pick up on cues that suggest something might be wrong or troubling them.

- Children may be fearful, anxious or embarrassed about the abuse they are experiencing.
- Children may not understand that abuse or neglect is wrong or harmful and that they should tell anyone about it.
- Children are emotionally attached to their abusers and feel that they are betraying them if they disclose.
- Sometimes children know that the consequence of disclosure may result in a change of circumstance or situation that they don't want to take place even when the abuse is harmful.
- Children are sometimes told to keep secrets or threatened by an abuser if they speak out.
- Finding a trusted adult or someone a child considers to be safe to talk to may take time or indeed not happen at all until a child is older or becomes an adult.
- Some children may not speak out because they believe that nothing will change should they do so.
- Children with English as an additional language may find it more difficult to communicate and therefore do not attempt to disclose abuse or neglect.

Children and young people who lived in households where domestic abuse, parental substance abuse and mental health issues were key themes to their abusive experiences were asked what had stopped them from speaking out. The Children's Commissioner for England (2018) reported that 'children often become experts at hiding what is happening at home'. Some older children who had suffered abuse over long periods of time and were therefore able to articulate their experiences commented on the reasons for non-disclosure. One 11-year-old girl didn't speak out initially because she was told by her parent, 'don't be telling anyone, whatever happens in the house stays in the house'. Another explained that she didn't speak out because she was fearful stating, 'I don't know what will happen with the words that I say and where it will go so it takes me a long time to trust someone'. There are lots of reasons as to why children will not speak out and early years practitioners should be mindful of the obstacles and circumstances that may lead to non-disclosure with the children they work.

TIME TO REFLECT

Think about the children in your setting. What might prevent them from being unable to communicate with you should they be experiencing abuse. How might you compensate for this and provide ways for them to express their feelings and communicate?

What is disclosure?

Disclosure is referenced in the Early Years Foundation Stage as 'children's comments which give cause for concern'.(DfE 2021). Children might say something briefly using few words or engage in full conversation if they disclose. When I speak to early years practitioners about their own experiences of disclosure, many recognise that younger children often use a sentence or two with brief moments of disclosure and then off they go to continue in play or return to the activity that they are engaged in. Sometimes children will open a conversation and not necessarily finish it. Older children may want to tell a trusted adult lots of information that involves holding a conversation over a longer period.

It is helpful to break down the process of disclosure for practitioners to consider how to respond and act because of a child's disclosure. This process includes, *responding, recording* and *reporting.*

Being in the moment

It can feel quite daunting for a practitioner when they realise that a child is telling them something as important as a disclosure of abuse or neglect. An out of school manager once described the feeling to me as 'being like a swan', outwardly calm and gliding over the water mindful not to react or panic in front of the child whilst staying calm and collected. Inwardly she said she was 'paddling like mad under the water' with her mind racing towards what she realised was happening and what she needed to do and how she should respond in order to achieve the right outcome for the child.

Being in the moment places the child at the centre of disclosure and involves the following.

- Listening carefully.

It might be difficult given where or when a child decides to disclose. It is always important to listen and take time to hear what the child is saying or communicating. Try not to react, appear shocked or give the impression that what the child is saying is unthinkable or unbelievable.

Responding in the moment

- Always give a child time and attention.

Think about your body language, does it demonstrate openness and encouragement from the adult's perspective that makes the child feel safe and listened to?

- Allow the child to give a spontaneous account.

Make sure that you don't jump in too quickly by trying to make sense of what is happening or trying to clarify what the child is saying to you before they have finished speaking. Disclosure may happen incrementally and not necessary all happen all at once.

- Don't offer false confidentiality.

Never agree to keep secrets or say that you won't tell anyone else if a child asks you to do so when disclosing. Always explain that you will have to tell someone else in order that something can be done to help them or keep them safe.

- Offer reassurance.

Children may need adults to reassure them that they have done the right thing by speaking to someone about their experiences. Children need to know that we are taking them seriously should they disclose. They need to know that we care about them and want to help them. They need to know that abuse is not their fault.

Recording

* Respond with accurate and timely record keeping.

If a child uses language and words that are unfamiliar to a practitioner or describes something to them, it is important that they recollect and record exactly what is said by the child in the child's own words without adding opinion or interpretation. It is important to record this as soon as the opportunity arises when the details are clear and fresh in mind; this way they can be recalled with clarity.

Reporting

* Always report disclosure of abuse.

Details and information about abuse through disclosure should be reported to the designated safeguarding lead in your setting immediately. If a practitioner is the designated safeguarding lead, they will consider having a conversation with statutory services where appropriate.

* Don't speak to the alleged abuser unless advised by social care to do so.

If on seeking advice from social care, practitioners are encouraged by to seek clarity or ask questions of a parent, make sure that this advice is recorded as such. If it is considered that by speaking to parents about abuse compromises that safety of the child or puts them at further risk for example in the case of sexual abuse, a practitioner should be confident to challenge this advice.

Do not attempt to investigate allegations of abuse against a child, this is the role of statutory services. If other professionals begin to ask questions and attempt to gather facts themselves, this may place the child and other children at risk. It may also prevent processes such as child protection enquiries from taking place, allowing the abuse to continue to the child in question and other children with whom the accused perpetrator comes into contact.

If a child speaks out about abuse, discloses something to an adult or makes an allegation of harm against someone, it is vital that we always respond from a child-centred perspective and ensure that actions during and following a disclosure focus on the needs and wellbeing of the child.

Making professional judgements

There are a whole range of elements needing to be considered when making professional judgements that in turn lead to actions to help and protect children. We must remember that everyone working with children has a responsibility to safeguard them and this cannot happen without applying some element of consideration, having thoughts or feelings about the situation. Whilst early years practitioners such as those who have the designated safeguarding lead role are required to apply the highest level of scrutiny, ultimately, everyone makes judgements in one way or another. Making professional judgements is the not the same as being judgemental; we need to be clear about this. Effective safeguarding practice requires judgement to be one of it's essential drivers.

Experienced and skilled practitioners can draw upon lots of things that influence their actions. They need to be *intuitive, analytical* and *decisive*.

Intuitive

How often have we heard or used the phrase 'something doesn't feel right to me', or 'I just have a feeling that won't go away'? We are often reluctant to use emotional responses or consider feelings in safeguarding contexts when in fact we should be using them as part of the process that determines our response. Munro (2020) talks about intuitive reasoning that works hand in hand with other approaches such as analytical thinking when making judgements. She also believes that 'the centrality of empathy and intuition needs to be acknowledged' in child protection practices and that it should be seen as a guiding aspect towards our considerations. Munro states that intuition can be 'articulated' and the 'ability to use it can improve with practice'. If we return to the topic of neuroscience and understanding brain function, we can see the interconnectivity of the neocortex – the reasoning part of our brain – and the subcortex – the emotional reasoning part of the brain. Both are inseparable, supporting the theory that intuitive reasoning is no less important than other processes that inform judgements, decision making and drawing conclusions. Munro draws upon the work of Hammond (2007), who uses sailing as a useful image to help understand the relationship between reason and emotion. Hammond describes reason as helping to 'steer the boat, but emotion provides the destination'. Intuitive and emotional responses offer a pre-requisite for additional and important safeguarding actions that enable practitioners to pursue other aspects of effective practice. This includes:

• Applying professional curiosity and finding out more about a situation.
• Responding and acting with a sense of urgency for the sake of the child.
• Becoming fearless in an approach to keep children safe or protect them, sometimes at the expense of practitioners' own positions and reputation.
• Demonstrating tenacity in the endeavour to meet a child's needs or go the extra mile.
• Challenging the status quo or going against the grain if practitioners believe others are not responding appropriately to a concern they have about a child.

Analytical

Analysis of a situation or circumstances for a child is something that is done constantly and sometimes without even realising it. Asking questions, pondering upon an uncertainty, or critically thinking about or examining a response from a parent who fails to reassure us about a child's safety all require levels of analysis. Early years practitioners will draw upon several things when analysing or pondering upon a situation that in turn informs their decision making.

Time to analyse – a scenario

What factors in Sarah's scenario would you use to analyse her situation? What are the things that stand out as concerning and are compromising her safety?

Sarah is three years of age and is one of four children living with Mum and her siblings in Grandma's home since the family were evicted from their property. Sarah's Mum has some learning difficulties and has a history of post-natal depression for which she takes medication. Staff at nursery often note that Sarah comes to nursery 'dirty and unkempt' and that she has recently lost weight. Her attendance is inconsistent, however when she does attend her nursery sessions, she eats snacks and food very quickly and has been seen to take food from other children at mealtimes.

Applying analytical approaches to bring together the main risk factors for children draws upon the features that give us most concern and that draws conclusions on the level of need for a child, which then informs our next steps. Analysis helps highlight the issues that require us to take action helping to determine what exact and appropriate actions are needed.

Decisive

Effective safeguarding practice requires confident practitioners to make the right and appropriate decisions about a child. Whether the decision is simply to follow a procedure and pass on a concern, or to return to something that intuitively we believe is worth taking further. Whatever the decision, be it small or large in consequence, it is worth reflecting upon what we need to inform our decision-making actions.

Being clearsighted about a situation will determine a number of things.

Asking the right questions:

- What do we already know? Is this sufficient information in itself to inform our decision making?
- Do we need to find out more and who will provide us with the relevant information needed in order to bring clarity or focus?
- Will the process of clarification or gathering new information involve fol-lowing information sharing practices that engage other professionals and therefore require consent from parents?

Effective decision making can be both independent and collaborative. I was hugely disappointed when a childminder seeking information from a health professional about a child in their setting when asking for clarity was told 'I can't possibly comment'! We need each other to help with decision making, this is the whole purpose of joint working. Collaborative practice at all parts of the process is a powerful and necessary strategy and should be seen as such by every professional working with children.

It is important however to note that practitioners do not need to have the full picture before deciding to act in one way or another.

Effective record keeping

Record keeping, especially when gathering evidence or information over time, is an invaluable tool to use to inform decision making. It is another effective safeguarding action that early years practitioners should frequently engage with.

What should be recorded?

Whilst there are no specific or definitive lists of things that practitioners must record as such, it is good practice to make note of various points that help ascertain or monitor a situation.

- Signs and indicators of abuse or neglect such as bruises, injuries, child disclosures or changes in a child's behaviour.
- Conversations with parents or other professionals that raise concern.
- Injuries a child may receive outside of the setting with dates and times of when they occurred, including explanations and reasons given by parents as to what happened and who was with the child at the time of injury.
- Absence from the setting and reasons given for the absence. In addition to noting times of absence and a record of what the setting did to establish contact with the child to ensure that they were safe and well. Any further actions taken in the light of any outcomes.
- Inconsistencies in care for a child such as frequent changes in adults given responsibilities to bring or collect them from the setting.

It is useful to think about the outcomes that efficient record keeping will offer practitioners. Recording provides an invaluable means by which to inform and manage other important safeguarding processes. Effective record keeping enables many things.

- A clear evidence-based process that provides important information about a child over time.
- A chronological record for gathering information or monitoring a situation or actions taken.
- Supports practitioners to make professional judgements.
- Assists information sharing.
- Provides information that can be used as part of a referral.
- Documents strengths, positive outcomes and changes in a situation.
- Provides a means by which to support and monitor progress or lack of parental engagement.
- Records can be used as an effective way to compile and write reports for multi-agency meetings and processes.
- Serves as a source of evidence for legal proceedings.

TIME TO REFLECT

Think about your systems for recording. How enabling are they in helping you and others focus on children's lived experiences? How do they inform actions to safeguard or protect children?

When considering intuitive, analytical, and decisive actions here are three important things to think about.

Think . . .

1 Patterns

What do patterns tell us about a situation? Patterns that show similar or the same adverse outcome for a child that are repetitive and frequent should raise concerns. Analysing patterns help practitioners to recognise things such as notable changes in a child's behaviour or wellbeing that manifests every other week or similar. A child may be anxious, afraid or hungry after spending time with different parents or significant adults such as parents' partners or older children living in the household where the child resides for part of the time.

2 Jigsaws

What pieces of the jigsaw do we *already have* in terms of information or knowledge about a child? What pieces of the jigsaw do we *need* to be aware of to build a clearer picture that will inform decision making or taking decisive actions that could safeguard or protect a child?

3 Chain reactions

What might happen as a result of an incident or circumstance that could trigger significant risk or potential harm for a child? A child whose family becomes homeless and moves into a household with unsuitable adults or young people placing them at increased risk. Or a parent whose mental health is in substantial decline and confides in a practitioner that they cannot cope.

TAKING DECISIVE ACTION
SHOWCASE – TAKING ACTION TO SUPPORT
PARENTS AND PROTECT CHILDREN

This showcase provided by a nursery shows the importance of strong relationships between parents and staff, enabling parents to reach out for help and support when they are struggling. Decisive action taken by the nursery not only served to protect children in the short term it also led to improved outcomes for the wider family in the long term.

Working to support Mom

Mom lives on her own with her four children, one of which attends the nursery. One day she approached the nursery manager asking if she could speak with her. Mom became very emotional explaining that she wasn't coping at home and that she needed support to keep her children safe. She went on to describe an incident where someone in the neighbourhood had set fire to her front door and this along with other threats from neighbours was placing their family in great danger.

Taking action – the nursery manager's response

After listening and consoling the troubled parent, the manager reassured Mom that she would do all she could to help her and offered to speak with the social care team to request their support. A very thankful Mom left the nursery and awaited a call from social care.

On investigating further, social care identified the extent of needs for this family and children warranted ongoing support from them. A plan was put in place and along with the nursery support was given to Mom and all four children. Things seemed to be moving in the right direction. However, through conversations between the nursery and social care it soon became apparent that Mom was not being completely truthful about her willingness to engage or change. She had repeatedly missed appointments with social care and was neglecting the medical needs of her children. Furthermore, evidence had emerged that she was using drugs herself, which compromised the safety of the children. The extent to which she had lied and shown disguised compliance towards professionals contributed towards the decision by social care to remove all four children.

Working to support Dad

All children moved to live with Dad and the nursery built an excellent relationship supporting him to gain custody of his children and helping with the ongoing engagement in respect to his child attending the nursery. The setting noted such a difference in the child; they presented as clean, calm, and happy and all their needs were being met by Dad.

The outcome

Mom moved into a new area and has begun to turn her life around. She is engaging in court processes and meetings around the care and wellbeing of the four children.

TIME TO THINK

The showcase demonstrates several actions taken by the nursery to make sure that their practice centred on the child's needs. What actions can you identify and how did they contribute to the process and final outcomes for the children concerned?

Taking action to protect a child
Making a referral to social care

If it is deemed that a child requires support or protection because of recognising significant harm, a referral to social care should be made by the designated safeguarding lead. The family should be informed of the referral except in instances of sexual abuse, fabricated illnesses, forced marriages or female genital mutilation and where if doing so would place the child at increased risk of significant harm.

A call to social care will help establish some important information or details that should be considered when making a referral. Social care can advise and help practitioners to achieve clarity on a situation.

Some things to consider when making a referral:

- Always clearly state the reason for the referral.
- Communicate the needs of the child as central to the process.
- Draw upon knowledge of the child and their circumstances.
- Use or apply thresholds of need (where relevant) to support the referral.
- Use professional judgements to inform decision making.

Professional challenge and escalation

Early years practitioners especially those with safeguarding lead responsibilities will sometimes need to take actions to challenge other professionals and escalate concerns that others have not deemed to be as high as they believe them to be. We will explore this further in chapter 6 when considering multiagency work and practices.

Key messages from chapter five

- Taking action to safeguard and protect children involves a whole range of things including making decisions, professional judgements and drawing upon conclusions.

- It is important for practitioners to understand differing levels of needs for children and know how to respond to them.
- Effective safeguarding practice involves knowing how to respond to a child's disclosure of abuse or neglect.
- Professional judgements are informed by intuitive reasoning; they require analytical approaches and informed decision-making processes.
- Actions taken to help or protect a child should always centre on meeting their needs and/or ensuring their safety and wellbeing.

Figure 5.1 This is what I feel like if no one listened to what I have to tell them.

References

Child Protection in England. (2022). *The National Review into the Murders of Arthur Labinjo-Hughes and Star Hobson*. The Safeguarding Practice Review Panel.

Children Act 1989. (1989). *Legislation*. Gov.UK (legislation.gov.uk).

Children (Northern Ireland) Order. (1995). Gov.UK (legisltation.gov.uk).

Children's Commissioner for England. (2018)."*Are They Shouting Because of Me*"? *Voices of Children Living in Households with Domestic abuse, Parental Substance Misuse and Mental Health Issues*. Children's Commissioner for England.

Children and Young People (Scotland) Act 2014. *Legislation*. Gov.UK (legislation.gov.uk).

Department for Education. (2021). *The Statutory Framework for the Early Years Foundation Stage: Setting the Standards for Learning, Development and Care for Children from Birth to Five*. Department for Education.

Early Intervention Foundation. (2018). *Releasing the Potential of Early Intervention*. Early Intervention Foundation.

Early Intervention Spending in England. (2022). *Too Little, Too Late*. Action for Children.

Getting It Right for Every Child. London: Scottish Government.

Hammond, K. (2007). *Beyond Rationality*. Oxford: Oxford University Press.

HM Gov. (2018). *Working Together to Safeguard Children. A Guide to Inter-agency Working to Safeguard and Promote the Welfare of Children*. HM Gov.

The Independent Review of Children's Social Care. (2022). Gov.UK.

Munro, E. (2020). *Effective Child Protection*. Third Edition. Sage.

The Munro Review of Child Protection – A Child Centred System. (2011). Gov.UK.

Safeguarding Children and Child Protection. *National Society for the Prevention of Cruelty to Children*. NSPCC Learning (Accessed 9.5.22).

Working with others to achieve the right outcomes for children. Parents and carers/multi-agency practice

Partnerships with parents and carers

Working in social care in the early 1990s I distinctly remember being aware of the power imbalance between professionals working with children and parents. Everyone was beginning to get their heads around new legislation. The Children Act 1989 significantly changed the way that professionals worked with parents. Its philosophy was that 'partnership and participation' should involve 'empowering children and families'. This meant that information should be shared with parents, and they were encouraged to be actively involved in decision making for their children. At this time, I recall conversations with colleagues about their concerns that they would now be expected to share their written reports about children with parents before meetings. Even more concerning to some practitioners was that parents would now have the right to attend meetings that had previously been held behind closed doors. The concept of partnerships with parents was flawed and one sided. It all sounds surreal that this even happened and that it wasn't that long ago. We've come a long way since then.

Developing meaningful engagement

Thinking back to the many parents I have worked with conjures up a whole mix of emotion and feelings. Some I still think about now; I wonder how they

DOI: 10.4324/9781003137054-6

are doing, what happened to their children some 30 years on. I along with other colleagues built strong and supportive relationships with parents and I know that without the help they received they would not have made such positive change or progress in their ability to look after their children. I love seeing this happening in the many early years settings I work with now. Early years practitioners offer a lifeline to so many parents and children and long may this continue.

I think it is important to understand the dynamics of relationships between practitioners and parents and the emotive responses that occur because of this. I have worked with some parents whom I disliked immensely for whatever reason, mostly because of the abuse they inflicted upon their children. I think that we need to hear the message that we don't have to like all parents, but we do in one way or another have to work with them. That is the challenge and a considerable one at that.

Understanding and appreciating the reasons why parents might find it hard to meet children's needs or if they seem unable to do so is central to developing relationships that enable meaningful engagement. It requires a number of things:

- **Empathy** and the ability to understand another person's feelings or reasons why they react or behave as they do. This can take time to really get to know the bigger picture or understand some background details that has led to a situation or circumstance.
- **Authenticity** and the desire to reach out to help change a situation that is genuinely motivated by wanting to achieve the right outcome for children and families.
- **Humility** and **compassion** and the realisation that not everyone's experiences will be the same neither will they necessarily be positive. Reasons for adversity and the effects of adversity should be viewed in a non-judgemental way. Practitioners working with families should appreciate their role as that of being able to advocate on behalf of someone who needs help.

Breaking down barriers, creating a place of belonging and setting boundaries

The first hurdle in relationship building with parents often involves reaching out to communicate a supportive and credible expectation or basis of the relationship, how it will form and grow. For parents who feel under confident or afraid because of personal experiences or difficult situations, practitioners may have to work a little harder and possibly longer to build trust. Parents may be suspicious or guarded when they are speaking with those who hold positions of influence, and it may take time for them to open up.

Belonging

When I worked in a Sure Start Local Programme I came across a young single dad and his two-year-old daughter. Tony had moved into the area to remove himself from friendships and relationships, including the mother of his daughter that had made it difficult for him to abstain from his addiction to heroin. He had achieved so much over time: he was no longer taking drugs, and his daughter was thriving, a true credit to him; he was an amazing dad. While his daughter started school, I became the manager in the newly built children centre on the school site. We became acquainted again and he started to come along to sessions in the centre. He was an incredibly talented artist and still struggling with the challenges of being a lone parent; we invited him into the centre each day to paint. He benefitted from the company of staff and other parents, and it meant he could work on his latest project – a piece of art that depicted his hopes and aspirations for his daughter. The painting captured the details of the children's centre, our staff team and the work we were doing, but most importantly it represented all that he wished for his daughter as she grew up. It was phenomenal and he gifted it to us to hang on the wall of the centre where it stayed until it closed some years later. What Tony needed was a place to belong and to be accepted by the people around him. A few years ago, I came across him on the streets of my hometown selling his paintings. He openly told me that he was not in a good place. He was taking drugs again and his daughter had been taken into care. He knew that he had failed her and felt bad about it. He also knew that he could be open and honest with me and that I didn't judge him in the light of what had happened. I haven't seen him for some time and often wonder how he is or what happened to him. With the help of colleagues, we were able to get Tony's painting from the children's centre and pass it to his now teenage daughter.

It is important that we invest in relationships with parents when outcomes are both good and bad, recognising that progress is not always a linear process and is often one with lots of twists and turns.

Setting professional boundaries

Whilst recognising that relationships with parents in early years are quite unique and provide beneficial qualities not always evident in relationships with other professionals, practitioners need to consider setting clear professional boundaries from the very start. Professional boundaries should be well defined and identifiable in that they are centred on children's wellbeing and protection. Parents need to understand the context of expectations or actions that practitioners will fulfil as part of their role and in regard to their safeguarding responsibilities. Practitioners should therefore help parents to;

- Understand that the relationship is respectful and supportive but is not based upon friendship even if practitioners are friendly in their approach.
- Have a clear expectation of the settings safeguarding policies and procedures and how these are applied and when.
- Appreciate that concerns that lead to actions taken by practitioners will be shared with appropriate agencies outside of the setting where appropriate.

From personal experience, as relationships between practitioners and parents develop and deepen, boundaries often need reiterating and re-establishing every now and then.

TIME TO REFLECT

How do you create a sense of belonging for parents whose children attend your setting? What does this achieve for parents, practitioners and most importantly the children?

I recently visited a nursery whose partnerships with parents was exceptional. Their approach was evident across the whole nursery; however, I was particularly encouraged to see that they engaged with the Operation Encompass initiative. A national initiative that has been adopted across the nursery's local authority, Operation Encompass supports victims of domestic abuse. Partnerships between schools, early years settings and the police facilitate information sharing, alerting a setting when an incident involving domestic abuse occurs in the home of a child attending the setting. When a setting is notified about an incident it allows practitioners to place the child in sight of the situation and offer the support that they need. It also means that the setting can work with both child and adult victims of domestic abuse by signposting them to appropriate services. I asked the manager of the setting how the initiative formed part of a wider safeguarding strategy for them and how this impacted positively upon the lives of children and parents they worked with.

Nursery

RB: How long have you been working with the Operation Encompass initiative in your setting? What are the features or characteristics of the initiative that help you to deliver effective safeguarding?

N: We have been working with Operation Encompass (OE) for the past twelve months. The features of OE have encouraged me to become more informed about domestic abuse and to be more aware of the triggers of domestic violence. OE also highlights the families to us that we have not previously had concerns about, and it gives us the opportunity to help and support them during a difficult time.

After I had received the training from the local authority, I cascaded this information to my staff team during a staff meeting. This helped them all to become more familiar with the statistics and signs of domestic abuse and what to do if they had a concern or had to handle a disclosure.

I then displayed the OE information in the nursery entrance, so parents are aware of the initiative, and I include an information sheet on this in our welcome packs.

The information displayed is a daily reminder to staff and parents that domestic abuse is happening around us and we need to be aware of this. Along with this I have posters about domestic abuse and help centre numbers displayed that parents can tear off and take away if needed.

RB: How does this initiative support children who experience domestic abuse and what experiences have you had as a result of being part of the OE strategy?

N:

- After an OE referral, practitioners are aware of the domestic abuse so they can support children quickly after an incident has happened at home.
- We can be aware of the behaviours that children are displaying and have implemented strategies to help them to cope with the situation. For example, we provide a quiet space for a child who needs time to regulate their feelings; they have a safe space to go to with their key worker.
- We provide 1–1 activities to support a child's emotional health and well-being – such as reading stories to the child or providing wishes and feelings activities.
- We make early help referrals to other professionals to get advice to support the child.
- We teach our very youngest children about healthy relationships – we read stories that are age appropriate.
- We provide children with at least one key worker with whom they can build a strong trusting relationship.

RB: How does OE help parents who are experiencing domestic abuse and how have you been able to support them to make good choices or decisions about their children's welfare?

N: OE gives us the opportunity to support parents sensitively. Once we have been given the information from OE we speak to the parents in a quiet place, which gives them the opportunity to talk about the incident and reflect on what happened. During this time, we ensure that the parent knows we are there to support them in a non-judgemental way and we always aim to build a trusting relationship with them. Many of our children are from dysfunctional family situations and much of the advice we give is around relationships with their partner and their children. The children involved in OE usually have poor attendance and we work closely with the parents to keep them in nursery consistently. We encourage parents to bring their children into nursery by offering free dinners, free uniforms and ongoing support.

We contact the parents within half an hour if they have not arrived in nursery; by being consistent with our approaches parents make the right choices to bring their children to nursery, which keeps children in a daily routine.

Principles of working with parents whilst maintaining a child-centred focus

The basis upon which we build effective relationships with parents must always consider what is best for the child. What we achieve through these relationships will of course indirectly impact upon children. Relationships should therefore be:

- honest and trustworthy,
- transparent and clear,
- respectful and considerate.

These principles ideally will form the basis of a reciprocal relationship. In reality, and for many reasons, this is not always possible when working in some contexts. Sometimes parents will intentionally act to avoid challenge or scrutiny offered by a professional. They may deviate from the issues being raised or hide the truths about abuse or neglect. In this instance practitioners need to remain focussed. It is easy to become distracted with the needs of parents or other adults in the lives of children and in doing so fail to place attention on the needs of the child. This can be made more difficult when working with parents who are manipulative and deceptive.

Disguised compliance

The term disguised compliance describes what is happening when parents or carers 'appear to co-operate with professionals in order to allay concerns and stop professional engagement' (Reder et al. 1993). Disguised compliance can manifest in various ways. The showcase in chapter five included examples of mom's actions that demonstrated she was telling professionals one thing and yet doing another. She gave the impression that she was attending important appointments when she was not attending them at all. The impact of a parent's dishonesty and a refusal to engage with interventions serves only to increase the risks that have already been identified as being harmful to children. It can be difficult to recognise that disguised compliance is occurring especially if multi-agency partnerships are not as effective as they could be. Information sharing between professionals who are working with children and families is essential for so many reasons, however to recognise disguised compliance multi-agency practitioners need to maintain regular contact and frequent communication with each other. Ongoing professional discussions will therefore help to determine a range of things:

- Inconsistencies in explanations or accounts of incidents and actions taken that involved the parent or carer.
- Accuracy in terms of parental expectations that have been agreed as part of early help, child in need or child protection plans.
- The use of other professionals to apportion blame or use as an excuse for not doing or doing something. Sometimes professionals can be used by parents to manipulate a situation and cause confusion meant to distract from a parent's behaviours and actions.

Professional discussions should enable updated analysis considering any new or developing information that may change a situation, such as recognising a child's escalating needs and what needs to happen next.

Working with parents – strength-based approaches and models

When working in partnership with parents or carers, it is important that we reflect and consider the strengths and positive aspects that demonstrate a parent's ability to provide positive outcomes for children and the extent and level to which this happens. Recognition of protective factors however small should be acknowledged and reflected in engagements and interactions with parents and included in overall analysis of a situation. When strength-based principles and approaches underpin our practice, parents are valued in so much that their contributions matter and their opinions are heard even if not always acted upon. Not only is this approach a respectful and appropriate way to engage meaningfully with parents, it also acts to ensure ongoing engagement when there are risks of disengagement or hostility towards professionals by a parent. We have to think of the bigger picture, this being the child. Strategies that ensure the end goal, to keep a child safe and protected, add value to policies and procedures and are inclusive of professionals' attitudes and approaches.

Signs of Safety, a strength-based approach to child protection, has a familiar model adopted by many local authorities (https://www.signsofsafety.net/what-is-sofs/). The approach developed in the 1990s by social workers in Australia and now used on an international scale, focuses on the question 'how can the worker build partnerships with parents and children in situations of suspected or substantiated child abuse and still deal rigorously with the maltreatment issues?'. Investigation and consideration of risk consider

- family and individual strengths, and
- 'periods of safety and good care that can be built upon to stabilise and strengthen a child's and family's situation'.

Assessment of risk consider three factors that help to assess danger, strengths and safety. The Signs of Safety assessment protocol is captured in a one-page framework that asks professionals to determine what they are worried about, what's working well and what needs to happen. During processes where decision making takes place such as child protection conferences, multi-agency professionals are asked to make s on the extent of a child's safety by using a 1–10 scoring activity.

Working in partnership with parents offers credible and collaborative ways to engage with them and is beneficial for the children in the short and long term. Strength-based approaches should be reflected in the following ways:

- Interactions and conversations with parents/carers.
- Information sharing and recording.
- Conversations with multi-agency professionals.
- Reports.
- Multi-agency meetings.

TIME TO THINK

Think about how you and/or your setting works with parents. What examples can you identify that demonstrate a strength-based approach towards safeguarding and protecting children? Are there areas where this can be developed further?

Understanding risk factors versus protective factors

I want to briefly re-visit the topic of risk factors mentioned in more detail in chapter four. This is because when we work with parents and carers, our knowledge of risk and vulnerability not only informs our overall practice, but it steers us to better understand the context of risk in light of known protective factors that parents are able to demonstrate. Case reviews inform us of the common themes that offer the most concern. Risks to children because of parental substance abuse, poor mental health or domestic abuse. The extra-familial threats outside of a family context such as child criminal exploitation, County Lines. The influence of another adult who is manipulating or controlling a parent and/or situation that causes harm to a child. Whatever the risks are and the reasons for these risks, consideration and analysis of identified protective factors must accompany our deliberations when making professional judgements about parents' ability to keep children safe.

For example:

A young single mother who has a two-year-old child lives in temporary accommodation. She and the child has moved from their home to flee from a violent relationship perpetrated by the child's father. Mom has several vulnerabilities herself including a learning disability, poor mental health and was previously a looked after child herself being taken into care on the grounds of neglect and emotional abuse. There is little family contact with the nearest relative, an aunt living some distance away.

We can identify immediately the main risks to Mom and acknowledge the extent of her vulnerabilities.

Protective factors that work to meet the child's needs may include:

- The child is well cared for, is clean and eats healthy and nutritious food.
- Regular medical appointments and development checks are kept and attended.
- Mom is taking prescribed medication to help with her depression.
- The child attends nursery and is making good developmental progress.
- The child's father in no longer in contact with Mom or the child.

TIME TO THINK

What changes to Mom's circumstances might impact upon increased risk for her child or compromise her ability to offer protective factors?

Adverse childhood experiences in parents

Parents who have suffered adverse childhood experiences may find it hard to be emotionally present for their children, due to their own unresolved trauma. This could result in blocked care (Hughes and Baylin 2012). This might include finding it difficult to be caring and responsive towards their child, particularly during times of need. Where parents struggle with self-regulation, this is likely to impact on their ability to co-regulate their children's thoughts, feelings and behaviour too. Once again case reviews recognise the catastrophic consequences for children due to actions or inactions by parents who have experienced trauma in their own childhood that deeply impacts upon their own children. Adults who have suffered adverse experiences as children may encounter:

- Poor mental health.
- Addiction.
- Difficulties in building healthy attachments with their children.
- Involvement in crime or criminal activity.

Working with fathers

Much has been spoken about regarding the lack of engagement with fathers of children who have known risks, especially estranged fathers. Professionals may not involve or engage them in processes, assessment or interventions that would otherwise offer protective elements for their children. Again, this is a common theme in case reviews. Whilst it is hard to engage with estranged fathers when we are working with children in our settings it is important that we seek information about a child's father where possible. It is helpful to understand the context of a relationship between them and the child's mother even if this may not be ongoing or positive.

Rule of optimism, being over optimistic

Understanding the *rule of optimism* as child protection concept is helpful when working in the early years. The term applies when professionals are over optimistic about a situation, potential positive outcome or level of risk or concern for a child. Choate (2019) states that the rule of optimism can sometimes prevent professionals from seeing 'what is really going on'. Professionals often misinterpret progress made, 'minimise areas of concern, focus mostly on strengths and ignore what is not working', leading to 'overly positive interpretations of what is going on'. Rule of optimism as a wider theme has greater complexities for statutory services who are ultimately responsible for assessment of a child's needs, however on reflection I think we can learn a great deal from understanding how being over optimistic can endanger children we are working with in the early years. The challenges of being too optimistic can be for various reasons.

- Our innate perspective is focussed on enabling positive outcomes for children and parents we work with. Sometimes making it difficult to balance any negative considerations.
- Relationships with parents can be longstanding, deep rooted and built upon genuine engagement driven by compassion and care that involves a level of emotional attachment.
- We don't want parents to think badly of us if we have to make disapproving, judgemental comments about them.
- We may not have all of the information about a situation and therefore cannot determine our judgement or assessment of risk accurately.

Sometimes we might work with others who are over optimistic about the safety or wellbeing of a child. Early years input and perspective can often challenge another professional's opinion or point of view.

SHOWCASE – NURSERY MANAGER

At a recent Initial Child Protection Conference, I was questioned and challenged by professionals who believed I had made an unnecessary referral to the specialist multi-disciplinary team that supports parents to build attachments and bonds with their children, for a mum whose child was attending our nursery. I reiterated that I had had a discussion with mum upon the child starting nursery when she had shared that she was a first-time mum with mental health issues and felt that the COVID-19 lockdowns had affected her ability to bond. Both the health visitor and the social worker disagreed with my reasons for referral and along with the Independent Reviewing Officer of the meeting they said that 'the bond between mum and baby has always been lovely'. Mum had told me that she supported my referral on her behalf and saw it as being 'the right thing' and was grateful 'to get any support she could'.

The specialist multi-agency team attended the meeting and shared that they had had a brief initial chat with mum and was not completely sure that she needed the service in full but there were elements that they could help her with. I felt like all the agencies were branding it unnecessary and I felt very awkward at the meeting.

Four days after the meeting an incident occurred which led to the child witnessing violence and where mum was under the influence of drugs. The police attended the incident and mum told them that she didn't care if the child was taken from her. The child was removed on an emergency Police Protection Order until they were able to place the child into the care of the child's father.

I feel that the way that other agencies viewed mum and her struggles were misunderstood and based upon limited and insufficient understanding of her needs. My concerns were upheld by the incident so I'm now hoping that professionals understand why I made the referral in the first place.

TIME TO REFLECT

When working directly with parents how do we establish risks that determine concerns for children? How might we communicate this with other professionals if their views or opinions about a child's safety are optimistic when ours are not?

Having difficult conversations with parents

Early years practitioners will relate to the challenges that come with confronting parents about situations or instances. Whether this involves constant reminders to meet a child's basic needs such as provide warm clothing in the winter months, breakfast before they attend day care, a reminder that the child really needs to seek advice from a GP because they are ill and so on. Having those difficult conversations including delivering unwelcome messages to parents requires skill and understanding on the part of practitioner. When because of ongoing communication failing to change a situation or in the light of ignored requests to parents to meet a child's needs, a planned and structured conversation is required. Here are some considerations that will help to support the process of having difficult conversations with parents.

- Understand what good communication involves.

Appreciate good and appropriate body language that is open and non-threatening or judgemental. Try not to allow emotions to get in the way of the message that needs to be delivered.

- Find somewhere appropriate to discuss the concern.

Privacy and sensitivity to the parents and the topic of discussion is vital. It might be difficult to facilitate a room that is free of distractions such as children being present especially for practitioners working on their own such as childminders. Ideally the conversation will take place somewhere that enables focus and concentration on the matters being discussed.

- Decide who will be part of the conversation.

Whilst not wanting to include other practitioners unnecessarily, – we do not want the parent to feel uneasy, overwhelmed or intimidated – sometimes it is advantageous to include other professionals. A child's key person or deputy manager may support issues where misinterpretation or deliberate false accusation by a parent is likely.

- Be prepared.

Prepare the parent by explaining that a conversation needs to take place. As and when this is done will depend on knowledge of the parent and topic for discussion. Take time to think through how as a practitioner you will conduct the conversation including how the parent might respond to the message. What will this look like during the meeting and what might happen next?

- Explain your concerns using factual evidence and information to support your concerns.

It is likely that the parent will have some ideas of what you want to talk about given the issues discussed leading up to the conversation. Refer to previous exchanges with them in relation to the issue. Use records of concern or details captured over time that help explain a situation and why this needs to be addressed.

- Explain your position as a professional working with the child.

You may have to re-establish professional boundaries or remind the parent of the settings policies and/or procedures in order to re-define the role of the setting in regard to safeguarding responsibilities and actions that might be taken in the light of a concern about a child.

- Provide clarity.

Clearly explain to the parent the reason for the conversation; 'I need to talk to you today because',. 'There's something really important that we need to talk about'. Explain exactly what it is you are concerned about. Don't deviate or make light of the situation. Offer clarity from the child's perspective and help the parent see the impact of their actions or inactions have upon the child. You might want to explain that a record of the conversation will be kept and agree with what this will include and that they can see what has been written. Be clear about what needs to happen next and what or who this will involve.

Back to Zara's story.

In chapter two I mentioned a parent I once worked with called Zara. All three of Zara's children were taken into care because of neglect. She struggled with addiction, and this impaired her ability to look after her children. The incident that led to action being taken by social care was because of severe medical neglect and her three-year-old daughter almost died. It was Monday morning and both the three-year-old girl and her one-year-old brother had been dropped off at nursery by mum. Within minutes of the children arriving staff recognised an infected injury on the girl's foot. Action was immediately taken, mom was contacted to ask about the injury, social workers were informed, and the little girl went to hospital where she stayed for several days being treated for sepsis. I remember the experience of all that was going through my head at the time when my hand hovered over the phone as I was about to call mom to tell her that she needed to return to nursery and that social care were on their way to take the children. I remember her arriving out of breath because she ran the whole way from home to the nursery in utter panic. Her face was ashen, and she was crying. The conversations that followed were difficult to say the least; everyone wanted a better outcome and one where the children would be able to remain with mom whilst kept safe and healthy, but this was not the reality of the situation. Fast forward four or so years later I was managing a children centre on a school site and there was Zara. She had worked hard to address her addictions and her mental health was improving. This meant that two of her three children had returned from foster care to live with her. Her daughter was now attending the school reception class. In an extraordinary circumstance, I was able to visit Zara at home. We talked about the day that the children had been taken into care and what that felt like. We both shed a few tears as we recollected the emotions involved at the time. Zara told me that as awful and regrettable the experience had been it was in fact the catalyst that caused things to turn around for her and the children. She acknowledged her gratitude to the staff in the nursery for acting as they did. She was now rebuilding her life again with her children.

Recognising the legal status of parents/carers

There can often be confusion about who has legal parental responsibility for a child. It is important for early years practitioners to understand the legal status of adults who have responsibility or guardianship for children.

Parental responsibility

UK law (Gov.UK) states:
A mother automatically has parental responsibility for her child from birth.
A father usually has parental responsibility if he's either:

- married to the child's mother, or
- listed on the birth certificate (after a certain date, depending on which part of the UK the child was born in).

An unmarried father can get parental responsibility for his child in one of three ways:

- Jointly registering the birth of the child with the mother (from 1 December 2003).
- Getting a parental responsibility agreement with the mother.
- Getting a parental responsibility order from a court.

Special guardianship orders

Some children may be in the care of an adult who has rights under a special guardianship order. If a child cannot live with their parents and adoption is not seen as suitable or the right option for them, people such as grandparents, relatives, or family friends with whom the child has a significant relationship can apply to a court to become special guardians to the child. The order enables guardians to make 'day to day decisions about the child' such as 'schooling and medical treatment without need to consult the birth parent' (Gov.UK).

Working with others to achieve the right outcomes for children – multi-agency practice

When professionals work in silos or fail to engage in joint working practices that holistically support the needs of children and families, poor outcomes will always occur. The lack of multi-agency contributions to assessment of risk in the cases of both Arthur and Star (Child Protection in England, 2022) were highlighted repeatedly in the national review into their deaths. Responses to referrals to social care in regard to Star, of which there were five, were considered to be 'significantly weakened by the lack of formal multi-agency child protection processes'. Decisions made by social care leading to inaction lacked input from others who knew Star and who were concerned for her safety. The report concluded that if strategy discussions had taken place with multi-agency representation this 'would have allowed professionals to put all of the evidence together, interrogate it, challenge each other's perspectives, and agree a coordinated and strong response'.

Most case reviews mention the shortfalls in multi-agency practice, and many will identify the lack of information sharing between professionals working with families as a significant and sometimes a catastrophic weakness leading to the death or serious injury of a child. I fear that the momentum towards effective multi-agency work that had gathered because of initiatives such as Sure Start Children's Centres has slowed down considerably. As one who was involved in developing and engaging with strategies that enabled better multi-agency work to take place, this is most disheartening and frustrating. I frequently hear about ongoing challenges and discrepancies in the early years sector that demonstrate we still have much to do and address in respect to how others perceive and value the incredible work done by the sector to safeguard and protect children. There is still very much a sense that early years practitioners are less experienced and knowledgeable about child protection matters and more so that practitioners input towards processes, particularly engagement with social care, can be seen as less important or relevant. The experiences of childminders and nannies suggest a more marginalised group, often dismissed as having little to offer in the wider context of decision making and contributions towards professional multi-agency engagement. In response to the growing concerns about ineffective multi-agency practice, recommendations made by the Child Safeguarding Practice Review Panel (2022) include developing 'multiagency agency child protection units' and establishing 'national multiagency practice standards for child protection'.

I appreciate that not all experiences of multi-agency practice will be negative for those working in the early years. However, I do see a trend that makes for much more challenging times to come. Practitioners should be confident and equipped to rise to these challenges and be reassured in their right to take a valued and important role around the multi-agency table.

What designated safeguarding leads say about their experiences of working with other agencies:

'This has been a struggle at times over the years that I have been designated safeguarding lead, at times feeling really inferior when around the table at multi-agency meetings and like a rabbit in headlights. However, having been involved in so many cases and the many years passing I have learned that nobody around that table is any more superior than I am when I am the one who sees that family the most!'

'Working in an area of high deprivation for several years has had it challenges, as designated safeguarding lead, I have benefitted from the advice of the local authority early years safeguarding lead who is always at the end of the phone to help with any problems that may arise and is always positive when supporting. As DSL's myself and my manager have gained confidence if we feel that the outcome for a referral needs to be challenged. Child protection conferences initially seemed daunting to attend but as I gained experience and confidence, I found it less stressful and worked with some wonderful Independent Review Officers whose knowledge and expertise still amazes me and I have been able to glean aspects of my knowledge through them.'

Key elements of successful partnership working

Gasper (2010) on consulting with children's centre leaders drew upon the 'key elements for successful partnership working as being grounded in shared values and visions strengthened by a number of principles'. He surmised several indicators for effective practice.

- 'All those involved are valued differing perspectives are respected, and skills, training and experiences contribute collectively.
- Change comes from the bottom up rather than the top down.
- There needs to be more encouragement of non-judgmental working.'

Additional reflections on effective multi agency practice identified the importance of practitioner's attitudes and values that encouraged important ways of thinking. Practitioners should therefore foster

- 'open mindedness, moving away from the all-knowing expert professional stance;
- the development of trust;
- adaptability and flexibility;
- the development of support that builds towards independency rather that dependency;
- the development of leadership that encourages flat hierarchies and distributed leadership (Hargreaves and Fink 2006: 82); and
- actively working to include all the stakeholders as equal partners.'

SHOWCASE – NURSERY

Child A was removed from the mother's care due to significant neglect. Child A had spent her first nine months strapped into a pushchair the majority of each day and most nights. This had impacted on the child's mobility and overall development. The child was placed into the paternal family's care. The family did not know about the child's existence until they were contacted by social care. The child went into foster care whilst a DNA was carried out to confirm the father's identity and a positive parenting assessment was completed. Dad, a young man in his 20s, became an instant parent and needed professional support to adapt to being a father to a nine-month-old child with significant development delays due to neglect. He worked full time and required day care with immediate effect.

The first social worker involved in the case was quite negative towards the child remaining in Dad's care and made it very clear that they were preparing a plan for the child's placement for when this arrangement failed.

Those working with the child in the nursery provided parenting strategies and a full programme of support for Dad and the child. We shared menus and recipes of the foods that child A liked to eat and that Dad could share with his Mom, the child's Grandma, to encourage her to eat at home. Child A's keyworkers supported Dad with sleep strategies and helped him to overcome the child's fear of pushchairs and cots. Child A was making good progress and her development was improving.

One morning Dad brought the child into the nursery, and it appeared that she had injuries to her head which looked like finger marks. Dad could not identify what the marks were, and he was told that we would have to report to the child's social worker. The social worker arrived at the nursery within the hour and booked a medical examination. As the child had severe separation anxiety a request was made for a keyworker to accompany the child to the medical examination. The social worker had arranged for a foster family to look after the child once seen by medics as she believed that dad was responsible for the injuries.

Dad met the team and child at the hospital and consistently defended any accusations of injuring the child that were being made against him. The outcome was that the injuries had been sustained by the bars of the child's cot whilst they were sleeping. The child returned home with Dad. Shortly after this another social worker was allocated to the child. Dad received further and consistent support and was awarded full permanent residency with his child.

As part of the wider multi-agency support given to Dad and the child, the nursery worked closely with Home Start and the child's health visitor who along with us acted as effective advocates for Dad. We all worked together to facilitate simple parenting support until the intervention was no longer needed and the child protection plan was closed.

3 key components for effective multi-agency practice

1 Support and challenge

It is essential for practitioners to build trusting working relationships with each other.

Each member of a multi-agency team should feel equally respected, valued and listen to. Their contributions should be welcomed and considered as part of the wider discussion and process.

Should differences in opinion arise these must be discussed, and appropriate actions taken. This includes following escalation or professional resolution procedures.

2 Teamwork

When working in a multi-disciplinary or multi-agency team, make sure that you understand yours and everyone else's role.

Discuss how you will work together to support a child or family, making clear the responsibilities apportioned to each member of the multi-agency partnership.

Always focus on and prioritise children's needs, placing them at the centre of all decision making and subsequent actions taken.

Think about other teams or professionals working with a child. Consider whether there is any information you can share that will help them provide support. Likewise, reach out to others who can offer you with the information needed to fulfil your role and responsibilities effectively.

3 Communication

Always be clear about what you are sharing and why.

Follow your organisation's child protection policies and procedures, which should set out how to share information, the reasons for doing so and with whom.

New proposals set out in the Child Protection in England (2022) report should see the development of a 'set of national operational standards for multi-agency child protection work going forward' (p. 114).

Challenge, escalation and professional resolution

There will be times when it is appropriate to formally challenge others who are part of multi-agency procedures if we believe that they are not working towards the best interests of the child. The importance of understanding and following local escalation procedures featured as a key learning issue reported in the NSPCC's (2021) learning from serious case reviews briefing that ana-lysed areas for improvement in early years safeguarding practices. Most local authorities should have an escalation policy that sets out reasons for its use and how to apply it in practice. The procedure enables differing of opinions or disagreement between professionals about decision making to be escalated to a practitioner's manager or, if need be, to those with overall oversight and responsibility for safeguarding within the organisation. Concerns that trigger the use of such protocols are usually due to not:

* recognising need or the signs of harm,
* accepting referrals for services,
* delivering services according to the LA's threshold of need, or
* sharing information about a child's welfare.

Some escalation policies include other areas of challenge for when profession-als do not:

* co-operate in delivering planned interventions,
* attend multi-agency meetings, or
* produce plans or minutes in a timely manner.

Information sharing

Sharing information between professionals must be done in ways that meet data protection law and principles. This will consider when consent from a parent is required and when because of safeguarding concerns consent is not required. Even when decisions are made to share information about a safeguarding concern with another professional without parental consent, it is always good practice to record the reason as to why the decision was made and the circumstances that led to the decision. A key feature in multi-agency practice is attending and engaging with various meetings where assessment of need is considered, and decisions are made as to the right actions needed to be taken as a result. Being confident enough to contribute to such meetings often comes with time. I remember my first child protection conference. I had wonderful support from my then manager who attended with me and sat next to me explaining what was happening and what would happen next. When it came to my turn to offer an option as to whether the child whom I was working with should remain on the child protection register (a term replaced with child protection plan) it felt daunting. It was the start of many attendances of meetings going forward but the support from a more experienced practitioner was really appreciated.

Early years practitioners may work alongside various professionals and people who are working with and/or supporting child in need of early help, child in need or child protection processes. This means that they will work with them to make decisions and create plans collaboratively to improve a situation for a child. This may include:

- Medical professionals such as general practitioners, health visitors, midwives, physiotherapists, speech and language specialists.
- The police.
- Social care.
- Early help services and family support workers.
- Schools and other early years providers.
- Housing.
- Voluntary bodies or charities.
- Foster carers.
- Solicitors and Guardian Ad Litem.
- Parents, adults with Special Guardian Orders and other family members.

Figure 6.1 My Mum makes me smile by Mei.

Early years setting may work with and attend children's review meeting for children in care and therefore will be expected to provide updates and relevant information about the child. They may work alongside professionals such as the Guardian ad Litem, someone appointed by the court to represents the child's interests or the Children and Family Court Advisory and Support Services (CAFCASS). This could be in relation to both child protection court proceedings and family court proceedings.

Key messages from chapter six

- Partnership with parents and carers must be meaningful and engaging in order to achieve the right outcomes for children.
- Relationships between early years practitioners and parents should be respectful and supportive.
- Sometimes we need to challenge parents when maintaining a child-centred focus and approach towards keeping their child safe and well.
- Adopting strength-based approaches whilst acknowledging the impact of known risks to children supports effective assessment of the child's needs.
- Effective multi-agency practice is built upon a reciprocal appreciation of each professionals' contribution, helping to keep practitioners' focus on the child.
- If a child's needs are unrecognised or not acted upon appropriately by professionals, this should be challenged, and the concern escalated to someone who can take further action.

References

Child Protection in England. (2022). *The National Review into the Murders of Arthur Labinjo-Hughes and Star Hobson*. The Safeguarding Practice Review Panel.

Choate, P. (2019). *The Rule of Optimism*. Swhelper The Rule of Optimism (swhelper.org).

Department for Education. (2022). *Keeping Children Safe in Education. Statutory Guidance for Schools and Colleges*. Department for Education.

Fullen, M. (2004). *Leading in a Culture of Change. Personal Action Guide and Workbook*. San Francisco, CA: John Wiley & Sons. Jossey-Bass.

Gasper, M. (2010) *Multi-Agency Working in the Early Years. Challenges and Opportunities*. London: Sage.

Hargreaves, A., and Fink, D. (2006). *Sustainable Leadership*. San Francisco, CA: Jossey-Bass.

Hughes, D.A., and Baylin, J. (2012). *Brain-based Parenting: The Neuroscience of Caregiving for Healthy Attachment*. New York.

National Society for the Prevention of Cruelty to Children. (2021). *Early Years Sector: Learning from Case Reviews*.

Reder et al. (1993). cited in *Disguised Compliance: Learning from Serious Case Reviews* (2019) National Society for the Prevention of Cruelty to Children.

The Children Act. (1989). *Legislation*. Gov.Uk.

What is Signs of Safety? Signs of Safety, www.signsofsafety.net. Accessed October 13, 2022.

Creating a safe culture – child-centred practice in the early years

How organisational cultures are established and developed

I have spent a lot of time studying and learning about leadership and management. This supported my work over time in various roles. I'm particularly interested in leadership models and what makes for effective leadership especially in an early years context. What really intrigues me is how cultures within organisations are established, what influences them for better and for worse and, most importantly, what cultures are conducive for organisations whose purposes and motivations have children at the heart.

What is meant by culture?

For the purpose of this chapter the focus on culture will consider the characteristics that feature in early years practice. The component **manage** is relevant to this theme whether this involves individual management of practice delivered by childminders and nannies or more complex management systems established in nurseries, groups or larger organisations. The word culture is defined in the Cambridge dictionary as 'the way of life, especially the general customs and beliefs of a particular group of people at a particular time'. Whilst this may be a generalisation of the word, I think that it very much fits into the description of what happens within work cultures

DOI: 10.4324/9781003137054-7

operating in the early years. How we perceive children and the extent to which our beliefs underpin attitudes and actions towards them is central when creating enabling, caring and nurturing environments that operate within safe cultures. Culture reflects the attitude, behaviours and expectations of people and the way that we think or reflect about something. It is important to note that culture doesn't just happen; it is created, grown and established over time. It requires a source from which it emerges and people to operate within it.

Leadership is key

Early years leaders have the power to create and influence the culture within their setting. Fullan (2004) recognises the requirement of 'moral purpose' for leaders who want to develop services that make a difference to the lives of others. He believes that 'whatever one's style, every leader, to be effective must have (and work on improving) moral purpose'. Our desire to achieve the very best for children therefore must be driven by a strong ethos that underpins everything we do to help and protect children.

Safeguarding toxins and nutrients

Influenced by the concept of leadership toxins and nutrients found in organisational culture, I began to think about what impacted up early years settings and what can be interpreted in relation to safeguarding toxins, the things that contribute towards poor outcomes for children, and nutrients, those things that benefit them.

Safeguarding toxins – the things that feed into negative cultures resulting in harmful and dangerous consequences for children.

- Putting adults needs ahead of the child.
- Not recognising or de-valuing the unique needs of children.
- Disregarding a child's wishes or feelings.
- Overtly poor behaviour towards children, both actions and spoken words.
- Unsupportive behaviour towards children.

- Lack of promotion of or ineffective equality and diversity practices.
- Complacency regarding safeguarding practices.
- Don't care attitude.
- Poor communication and not sharing information in a timely and appropriate way.
- Working in isolation.
- Not following the correct procedures.
- Refusing to be accountable to those in authority.
- Non-reporting.

Safeguarding toxins should be challenged and addressed by those who have children's wellbeing at the heart of practice.

Safeguarding nutrients – the things that feed a positive culture contributing towards safe and healthy environments where children's needs are prioritised and met.

- All practices, policies and procedures are centred on the child.
- People working with children acknowledge and respond to children's unique needs.
- Practitioners take time to actively listen, respect and respond where possible to children's wishes and feelings.
- Modelling supportive and respectful behaviour that nurtures and provides safe boundaries for children to develop and learn.
- Providing caring and loving interactions between practitioners and children that demonstrate safe and healthy relationships.
- Knowing, understanding and following procedures that safeguard and protect children.
- Applying professional curiosity and always pursuing concerns about a child's welfare.
- Sharing and receiving relevant information whilst maintaining confidentiality.
- Working with others to promote good health and effective safeguarding practices.
- Taking personal responsibility to help and protect children.

Safeguarding nutrients help to set standards and expectations for effective safeguarding practice to take place in the early years.

TIME TO REFLECT

What does the culture of safeguarding look like in your setting? What elements of practice ensure that children are safe and well?

TEAM TALK

Take time to talk with your team about the safeguarding toxins and nutrients. How do you combat the toxins and prevent them from happening? To what extent do the nutrients recognised in your setting support you to deliver safe practices for children.

When it all goes wrong!

Poor practice due to poor culture often paints a bigger picture. When unhealthy and dangerous cultures impact negatively upon children this usually involves more than one relevant factor contributing towards devastating outcomes. This poor practice is likened to cogs in a wheel that turn the whole mechanism around, influenced and shaped by ineffective leadership and lack of management oversight. In the same way that risks often escalate as circumstances and situations align leaving children open to further harm, the same chain reactions apply within cultures. One negative thing leads to another. If foundations are weak and the culture of a setting accommodates poor outcomes, we have big problems. Inspection reports, or regulatory actions taken by Ofsted or the Care Inspectorate, capture the extent by which dangerous practice soon becomes the dominant features within a setting. For example, an early years provider with two settings is inspected at one of their nurseries. They are judged to be inadequate in all areas because of serious safeguarding breaches and concerns. Ofsted identify several areas where children are placed at risk because of dangerous practices in the nursery. Failings mostly centre on weak management. The nursery has no deputy manager to act in the absence of the manager. Child ratios are not met. Health and safety breaches are apparent, fire exits are blocked and environments are unsafe. Poor hygiene is evident; children cannot attend to their own toileting needs because there is no toilet paper available to them. The inspector notes that babies in the nursery are distressed and not comforted by practitioners. Leaders and managers do not recognise the safeguarding risks due to staff's inadequate knowledge of child protection and the manager fails to fulfil their role as the designated safeguarding lead. Staff do not know how to follow procedures that they should engage in if an allegation is made against someone working in the nursery. Details in inspection reports that are judged inadequate always focus on significant safeguarding breaches. They consider the impact upon children and those that mention multiple failings are indicative of a culture that has lost focus on the child. Weeks later the second nursery owned by the same provider has a regulatory visit from inspectors due a concern brought to Ofsted's attention. As a result of this visit their registration is suspended because Ofsted believe that children may be at risk of harm. Their findings mirror those of the inadequate nursery.

It is incredibly hard to address cultural weaknesses that are embedded in practice and the extent to which attitudes and values must change in order to keep children safe. It is also very difficult to break the cycle of deficiencies in bad practice. I know from my own personal experience as a leader it requires **boldness** to address the issues and those who are poorly performing. It requires **tenacity** to bring about change and to stick with the plan until changes happen for the good of children and no one else.

Our actions and responses to cultural dangerousness will depend on our roles and responsibilities. It also depends upon our positions of influence, whether we are a manager of a setting and can bring about change or whether we work in a setting and must speak out against it. This sometimes includes whistleblowing if there seems no other option available.

Little Teds and Little Stars nursery case reviews

Learning from case reviews informs us a lot about poor culture and emphasises the importance to act to intervene in a situation where children are at risk because of behaviours, inactions or actions displayed by professionals who work with them. Some of the most shocking reviews detailing serious child abuse perpetrated by adults working in nurseries who committed crimes against children include those of Vanessa George and Paul Wilson.

Vanessa George worked at Little Teds Nursery, Plymouth and was convicted in 2009 of sexually assaulting children, taking photographs of the abuse on her phone and distributing the images amongst a network of pedophiles. She served just over eight years of a prison sentence for her crimes. The impact of the abuse and findings from the serious case review led to reforms of the Early Years Foundation Stage in 2012. We still see references to this case in the expectations that providers will manage mobile phones and cameras in early years settings. The nursery culture which enabled the abuse to take place was very much influenced by George's strong personality. She would bring pornographic images into work on her phone and use crude language. Colleagues struggled with her inappropriate behaviours but felt unable to speak out about this. They didn't know how to address the issues and the nursery manager did not share their concerns.

Not long after the incidents at the Plymouth nursery came to light, other sinister and disturbing revelations were emerging about child abuse in another nursery. Paul Wilson who worked at Little Stars in Birmingham was convicted of raping a three-year-old girl who attended the nursery and whom had been recognised by colleagues as having been singled out by Wilson. 'Concerns began to be expressed amongst the staff team about the "special" relationship that he had with the child' (Wannacott 2013). There were a number of colleagues who were troubled by Wilson's behaviours whilst not knowing the full extent of his abuse. However, it was students who had heard details of Wilson's engagement with the child who took their concerns to a college tutor who in turn passed them to the Local Authority Designated Officer for Birmingham's Children's Social Care. There were a number of failed attempts to investigate the true nature of what was happening at Little Stars Nursery. It wasn't until a police investigation centred on Wilson's sexual crimes against a teenage girl that Wilson confessed to the abuse of the three-year-old taking place in nursery. The review notes a number of unsafe and dangerous practices that were apparent in the nursery at the time.

- Safer recruitment procedures were not followed.
- Wilson began work without the nursery having proof of his qualifications; at the commencement of his employment the nursery believed him to be qualified but in fact he was not.
- Complaints to the nursery manager about Wilson's 'special relationship' with the child were made known to them but not addressed.

One thing stood out to me when I read the review some years ago. The author had interviewed Wilson as part of their research. Wilson explained that as a student he had not abused children in the school where he had been on a placement and had 'appreciated the clear rules that were in place'. The review concluded that Wilson 'made it clear that abuse would not have happened on another placement because of "rules"'.

Safeguarding policies and procedures that protect children from abuse, including from those who are sexual predators such as Wilson, are there to be followed and adhered to. They help form the basis of safe and protective practices that prevent children from harm.

TIME TO THINK

Consider the different policies and procedures in your setting that underpin safe practices. Do they cover staff conduct and behaviours? If so, what do they state?

Allegations against professionals or adults working with children

Knowing how to respond to concerning behaviours, observations or knowledge of harmful practices that impact negatively upon children is crucial for early years professionals. Allegations, or the belief that a child is exposed to harm because of adults working with them or those who are in a position of trust, need appropriate and timely responses.

What constitutes as an allegation?

The statutory guidance for schools and colleges in England (DfE 2022) differentiates between allegations that meet the threshold for harm and those that are termed as 'low level concerns' which won't meet the threshold. Whilst the guidance is relevant for school nurseries and not all early years settings, it is a helpful read.

Guidance determines that 'allegations' relate to a wider group of people working within the school and includes indirect employees or personnel such as supply teachers, volunteers and contractors. This aids the concept of including those who are in a position of trust and who might therefore be seen as having influence over children because of their role and association with the school or college.

Allegations that may meet harm thresholds include someone who has:

- Behaved in a way that has harmed a child, or may have harmed a child; and/or
- Possibly committed a criminal offence against or related to a child; and/or
- Behaved towards a child or children in a way that indicates he or she may pose a risk of harm to children; and/or
- Behaved or may have behaved in a way that indicates they may not be suitable to work with children.

Low level concerns

Allegations that do not meet the harm threshold should also be acted upon. To ensure an 'open and transparent culture' is promoted, 'all concerns about all adults working in or on behalf of the school or college' should be 'dealt with promptly and appropriately'. Lower level concerns must be addressed and opportunities taken by managers to consider any patterns or emerging themes in relation to the concern. It may be that actions follow including disciplinary or performance related conversations with the staff member. This not only addresses the concern but has the potential to prevent the concern from escalating to something more alarming.

Processes that follow an allegation

There are a number of things that can happen as a result of an allegation. Depending upon the nature of the allegation this can involve internal investigations, consultation with external bodies such as the Local Authority Designated Officer, England (or equivalent, such as The Scottish Social Services Council for Scottish providers). If the allegation indicates that a crime may have been committed this will involve reporting to and investigation by the police. Advice from human resource services will provide settings with guidance about how to manage situations that may require staff redeployment or suspension during an investigation. The advice will consider compliance with employment law and ensure that the employees' rights are upheld. For the alleged person, support can be given by their employer, unless advised otherwise, and if they have union membership, support and advice should be offered to them on the matter. Early years providers in England who are registered with Ofsted, or childminders with a childminder agency, must notify Ofsted or the agency of 'any allegations of serious harm or abuse by any person living, working, or looking after children at the premises'. This includes allegations that relate to harm or abuse on the premises or elsewhere'(DfE 2021).

Whistleblowing

Occasionally when practitioners find it difficult to engage in internal procedures regarding an allegation, they can take their concerns to an external body through whistleblowing. This usually happens when there seems to be no alternative option and if their concerns are not being addressed appropriately within their own setting or organisation. The National Society for the Prevention of Cruelty to Children has a national Whistleblowing Advice Line for anyone wanting to contact them.

The NSPCC Whistleblowing helpline is available via their website; www.nspcc.org.uk/keeping-children-safe/reporting-abuse/dedicated-helplines/whistleblowing-advice-line/
By telephone on 0808 800 5000 or by emailing them at help@nspcc.org.uk

SHOWCASE – RESPONDING TO AN ALLEGATION MADE BY A PARENT AGAINST A MEMBER OF STAFF. A NURSERY MANAGER'S EXPERIENCE

I have worked in the early years sector for eighteen years and have been a manager and safeguarding lead within a small chain of nurseries for 11 years. This is the first time that I have had to manage an allegation against a member of staff.

The allegation

I was approached by a parent of a three-year-old child who told them that their child disclosed over the weekend to them that 'a member of staff had smacked her legs whilst they had been on the toilet as she had been messing about with the toilet roll'. The child had indicated to them that it had been on the upper part of her left thigh. The child had attended the nursery for two and a half years prior to this and the nursery team had a good relationship with the family and there had been no previous issues. The child initially stopped attending the nursery but returned during the latter stages of the investigation.

What happened next?

I documented the discussion between myself and the parent and explained my next course of action. I explained that I would follow the company procedures that follow in an event where an allegation is made, and this included contacting our Local Authority Designated Officer (LADO) to tell them about the allegation and to seek advice on what I should do next. After speaking with the parent, I made a call to the nursery director to tell them of the allegation and to ask their advice. I knew that they would provide me with the support that I needed to manage the allegation.

Contacting the LADO

When I made initial contact with the LADO, I was asked to leave a message and the person on duty would contact me as the LADO was currently unavailable to speak to me. After a 35-minute wait, which felt forever, I received a call from the duty team who asked me to submit a referral to the LADO. They also told me to advise the child's parent to contact the police and report the allegation should they want to. I was told to speak with the staff member involved to say an allegation had been made against them but not to disclose any additional information to them about the allegation.

I made a telephone call to the parent explaining that we had taken advice from the LADO and that they had suggested the parent could make a police report if they wished to. The parents chose not to do this.

I completed a LADO referral and sent this to them.

Speaking with and supporting the alleged member of staff and the wider team

With the support of the area manager, a meeting was held with the team member involved to discuss the allegation. During this meeting the team member became distraught that an allegation had been made against them; we discussed that an investigation would take place led by the local authority and we would keep communication with them as transparent as possible whilst this was taking place. We also informed the team that as an additional safeguard for all concerned, they would work under supervision whilst the allegation was being investigated. The following day the team member arrived for work and went into their base room; it was evident that they needed further support and reassurance and another discussion took place to provide this. I explained that procedures had to be followed and that the confidential nature of the allegation would not be discussed with anyone other than those who needed to know about it.

What happened next in respect to the referral to LADO and how the parent was kept informed of progress made into the investigation of the allegation?

A series of calls took place between us and the safeguarding unit to check that they had received all the information they needed. Updates were provided to the parent, and they were happy with how the allegation had been handled and were also happy to be kept updated by the nursery each day by telephone.

The LADO requested further information from the nursery, including whether any previous allegations had been made against the alleged staff member, the length of time they had been employed, details of references when recruiting them and if anything had arisen during supervisions or peer observations of their work and practice. At this point I was offered further guidance on what I should do next. I was advised by the LADO to hold a meeting with the team member and give them a little information regarding the allegation. This information included the date and area where the alleged incident took place and the name of the child who had made the disclosure.

The LADO explained to me the next stage of the process. The nursery director and I would be invited to attend a strategy meeting. The parent and the team member would not attend this meeting, but we would be able to give feedback to them afterwards. A call to the parent to feedback the outcomes of the meeting was received well. They explained that their child would be returning to nursery the following week and they were pleased with everything that had been done so far by the nursery to address the allegation.

In keeping with further advice given to us, the area manager and I held a meeting with the alleged member of staff. Again, this caused upset to the team member and they were unable to recall any significant event that may have occurred between them and the child. Following this meeting, records of the conversation were sent over to the safeguarding unit as requested. During this time, we took the opportunity to review our policies ensuring that we were following the correct procedures and that the policies were effective and robust.

The impact of an allegation upon the alleged person and the wider team

The team, whilst sensing things were not quite as they usually are, went about their daily practice tending to the children needs and providing a happy stimulating environment with lots of enjoyable activities. The following day during a regular 'check in' with the team member, they explained that they felt drained. They were very emotional, and I could see this was affecting their own wellbeing greatly. The following day they called nursery to say they were unwell and had been unable to sleep, been vomiting throughout the night and were very distressed. I explained that I was here to support them and to contact me and if there was anything they needed.

What about the child who made the disclosure?

The child came back into nursery. On their first day back, they came bouncing through the door happy and eager to return to their friends. I noted that the parent was happy to drop their child off which gave me some relief.

The alleged member of staff

A day after the child returned to nursery the staff member called to say that they had been signed off work by a doctor due to the stress and anxiety that the allegation had caused. Again, support was offered to them from myself and the company. I explained that I would update on any outcome from the meeting that was scheduled to take place the following day.

What happened next and the outcome of the investigation

The following day the nursery director and I attended another meeting with the LADO; neither of us had been in this situation before and we were wondering what to expect. I felt a little on edge and unnerved not knowing what was going to happen. At the meeting along with others we looked at the allegation, the information about the team member's previous good character and any supporting evidence. In this instance it was deemed that no solid evidence was available, and that the allegation would be noted as unfounded.

After leaving the meeting I called the team member to check in with them and explain to them the outcome of the meeting. Even though the outcome of the investigation was unfounded, they continued to experience stress and anxiety. Again, I offered support but felt a little helpless.

The response from the parent

When the parent arrived to collect their child that day, I updated them with the meeting outcome and in their words, they said 'if I didn't think you would keep her safe, she wouldn't be here. I am happy with everything that was done but I do have to listen to my child'. The parent stated she was happy for the team member to continue working within the room and with her child. Following on from the allegation the child came back into nursery until she left for school. The family has kept in touch with the nursery.

Outcomes for the member of staff, nursery practice and the nursery manager

The team member returned after a period of absence; it took time working with them to build their confidence back to the level it was before the allegation was made. The practitioner's confidence did improve but they later decided to take a career change.

As a result of the incident, we changed the frequency of our staff supervisions from termly to monthly and room observations took place more often.

Since managing this, my first allegation, I have gained insight into the process and the procedures that followed, however a few months later when I had to deal with a separate allegation, I still got that gut wrenching feeling. I am thankful that I work for a supportive company, where I receive thorough supervision. I can discuss things that may be affecting me with the director or area manager. Support and guidance have played a huge part in helping me throughout these challenging situations.

I acknowledge that there will be examples of poor or dangerous practice in the early years resulting in children's safety or welfare being compromised. I also acknowledge that often accusations or allegations of harm against children can be because of misunderstanding, false information, untruths and sometimes malice. As a manager of early years provisions and services, I have experienced both scenarios. Professionals can sometimes be scapegoated, accused by parents or carers, deflecting their own actions upon people working with children in an attempt to hide abuse. This sometimes happens, especially in settings who are working with children and families with complex needs or where there are existing safeguarding concerns. As challenging as it may be to engage in process such as that in the case of the nursery manager who addressed the allegation, our motives and intent should always be directed towards the safety of children even if the fall out because of the situation causes distress and anxiety for adults who work with them.

Strategies that promote a child-centred culture

Adhering to safe working practices

Building upon the foundations of compliant practice, this being the minimum of expectations, other strategies will help to further strengthen early years practitioner's work providing optimum benefits and results for children. In this section of the chapter, I want to refer to both the legal requirements and best practices that support a safe, child-centred ethos when working in the early years.

Legislative requirements

In chapter three I drew attention to child protection legislation being informed by incidents or more to the point tragedies where failings to keep children safe were identified. The requirement within law that ensures children's safety regarding those people working with them are no different. The process of safer recruitment and all that this involves was strengthened and influenced by the findings of the Bichard Inquiry Report. The report instructed by the UK Home Secretary examined what had happened leading up to the conviction of college caretaker Ian Huntley for the murders of ten-year-olds Holly Wells and Jessica Chapman in 2002. Bichard's report published in 2004 made recommendations for change in the way that the children's workforce should be safely recruited. This included establishing systems for vetting the suitability of all persons working with children and vulnerable adults.

All early years practitioners should engage with:

Safer recruitment practices and procedures that demonstrate safe practice from the start including clear expectations in job advertisements, conducting effective interviews, obtaining references and suitability checks.

Effective *staff induction* processes that provide important information and expectations about safeguarding for new staff.

Ongoing suitability activities that provide not only self-declaration opportunities for staff who through actions, conducts or behaviours identify themselves as unsuitable, but that include observations and scrutiny from managers also.

Code of conduct

Creating and working towards clear expectations of what is expected from early years practitioners is important, always of course in the interests of children and as a by-product often for the benefit of adults too. Guidance from the Safe Recruitment Consortium (2022) supports adults working in educational settings such as the early years to 'establish the safest possible learning and working environments which safeguard children and reduce the risk of them being falsely accused of improper or unprofessional conduct'. This comprehensive guidance considers a wide range of important aspects of practice including:

- Making professional judgements.
- Power and positions of trust and authority.
- Confidentiality.
- Standards of behaviour.
- One to one situations.
- Dress and appearance.
- Social contact outside of the workplace.
- Intimate/personal care.
- The use of control and physical intervention.
- Photography, videos and other images/media.
- Duty to report concerns about an individual's suitability to work with children.
- Sharing concerns and recording incidents.

Whilst maintaining our focus and priority upon children, early years practitioners also must be mindful of how to keep themselves safe from accusations of wrongdoing. Working in a team can make this so much easier and addresses the vulnerabilities that working in isolation present to practitioners. It is so much more difficult for lone workers such as childminders and nannies. I know from working with both the difficulties when faced with accusations or when placed in a situation that may involve an allegation or complaint of wrongdoing.

Helpful strategies for childminders and nannies

Relationships with parents that are grounded upon professional expectations serve to provide a strong foundation that helps establish the context of the partnership between the practitioner and parents. Whilst operating from a home-based environment, clarity and an understanding that the home is also a workplace must be considered. More so for childminders, this will include appreciation from parents that the workplace is also often the practitioner's family home.

As well as developing and applying policies that reflect practitioners' legal responsibilities and duties, it is helpful to set some clear boundaries.

- Be clear about when working and operational hours start and end. This underpins and re-emphasises the relationship as based upon contractual expectations rather than friendships.
- Create an environment that is conducive to meeting children's privacy whilst offering transparency about meeting children's intimate care needs. For instance, having a policy that explains how nappy changing or intimate care is undertaken in the setting. This may include recording nappy changes or other similar activities that can be shared or communicated with the parent.
- Think about what content is shared on social media posts both on personal and/or business pages. Whilst this applies to all early years practitioners, lone workers are in a weaker position when it comes to false accusations. If for any reason the relationship between parents and practitioners becomes strained or awkward, privacy and protection of personal and family privacy is important to maintain. Once again, it draws a line between personal and professional profiles.

- Nannies working in family homes should make clear work time and non-work times. They should maintain privacy and set boundaries for bedrooms or places in the home environment assigned to them, making these personal spaces 'no go areas' for children they are employed to work with.

TIME TO REFLECT

If you are working as a childminder or nanny, what kind of things would you expect to consider in a code of conduct that relates to your work and working environment?

TEAM TALK

Identify the things that are expected within your team that refer to staff conduct. By following this code, how are children kept safe?

Using professional supervision to keep children safe and well

In 2011 Claire Tickell responded to a request from Government to revisit the legislative framework for early years in England. She made several recommendations some of which led to changes and a strengthening of a revised Early Years Foundation Stage statutory framework. Tickell believed that supervision should be 'intrinsic to effective leadership and management practice' and challenged the lack of understanding of what effective staff supervision should be. To address this, she recommended changes emphasising a focus upon 'reflective practice', moving away from the 'perception that (supervision) is merely a tick-box approach to check what practitioners are, or are not, doing'. A reframed expectation for supervision would become part of the wider strategy to improve practice in early years settings. From personal experiences of undertaking supervision both as supervisee and supervisor, it has always been a key feature in social care; supervision void of reflective practice is nothing more than just a chat between two practitioners and does very little to develop practice that advances chances for children. Once again working upon the premise that legislative requirements are the minimum basis upon which to build, a safeguarding culture will seek ways to go beyond this.

There are three areas that the Early Years Foundation Stage state should be used to provide opportunities to conduct staff supervision. Whilst supervision considers a wide range of topics, I want to focus on each area referencing some opportunities that can be taken when safeguarding and protecting children. Even if you do not work with the Early Years Foundation Stage, these areas are a helpful guide to aid effective staff supervision.

1   Discussing any issues – particularly concerning children's development or wellbeing, including child protection concerns.

In addition to other conversations that take place as and when concerns arise, supervisions should be planned and structured to talk through the individual needs of children. This may include identifying levels of need for those who require early help or early interventions so that they can meet developmental expectations if they are struggling to do so. It might include analysing information and sharing knowledge about a child or situation that collectively supports decision making and coming to an agreement on what actions should take place next. Discussions that involve intuitive reasoning that explores the feelings or emotions that arise from those working with children who are experiencing abuse or neglect are helpful during supervision ultimately for the child but also the supervisee. Opportunities to talk about colleagues or practices in the setting that may be a cause for concern will be extended from initial conversations to that of scrutiny or reassurance that actions taken by managers have had sufficient impact upon children's wellbeing and safety.

2   Identifying solutions to address issues as they arise.

Staff who are key persons to children subject to planned interventions including those on child protection plans (or equivalent) are supported to work with the child and identify areas of progress made. Areas of concern such as lack of parental engagement or delayed progress in achieving outcomes agreed in plans can be discussed further and strategies put into place to address this. An effective supervisee will appreciate the contributions provided by practitioners and work with them to explore their ideas. A solution focussed approach on supervision supports collaboration and shared decision making. Conclusions about how to achieve the right solutions or outcomes for children will emphasise and prioritise their needs.

3   Receiving coaching to improve practitioners' personal effectiveness.

Experienced supervisors provide practitioners with the essential skills that help them to become confident and competent within their role. They will encourage reflection and critical analysis by asking questions and exploring options and scenarios. Through the process of coaching practitioners will be supported to develop and build upon individual learning goals that strengthen their ability to identify when and how they can help and protect children. The learning process is a vital component where coaching is concerned. It recognises and acknowledges the incremental development of individual practitioners and supports their personal effectiveness. Coaching encourages supervisees to recognise areas of new learning they may need. It encourages and enables self-directed learning and inspires the pursuit for ongoing knowledge recognising that there is always something new to learn.

Trauma informed approaches and practice

I have already commented that as a practitioner years ago I would have benefitted tremendously by having knowledge of neuroscience and an understanding of the impact of trauma upon young children's brains. It would have helped me to think about behaviours and concerning traits exhibited in children and know best how to respond to them. I am encouraged to see significant progress made towards recognising the need to address responses and strategies that support children who experience trauma because of abuse or neglect. The emphasis upon trauma informed approaches and practice is growing and I believe this is something that every early year's practitioner should embrace and develop. Conkbayir (2021) believes that 'adopting a trauma informed approach will not only nurture the holistic and ever-evolving wellbeing of trauma survivors but will prove beneficial to everyone in the setting'. When practitioners use trauma informed approaches to support young children, they enable some important and key aspects that contribute to children's overall wellbeing. Conkbayir notes several attributes such as:

- Reframing behaviour.
- Increased co-regulation, which is vital for the development of self-regulation.
- Resilience.
- Stability.
- Sense of security.
- Sense of belonging.
- Creativity and imagination.

Early years practitioners can and do adopt simple and familiar strategies that help children who experience trauma. The relational role of the key person or the person with whom the child has meaningful attachment is fundamental. Extending the care and relational benefits beyond that of key persons is also most important. Settings where loving and nurturing relationships are consistently evident across the whole team will make the most impact. Some of the most wonderful experiences I've seen of this are where all adults, whether they are practitioners or not, are attuned to a culture that embraces children and respectfully interacts with them picking up on cues and knowing when and how to engage with them. Daily routines that offer a sense of consistency and expectation of what happens next help children to feel safe. Even the mundane routines of mealtimes, snacks and planned or structured activity can bring calm and certainty when children are otherwise experiencing distress and insecurity. Children who experience trauma need to be supported by practitioners who understand child development and self-regulation. They need to appreciate that trauma derails the ability for a child to self-regulate their emotions and they must learn how to support them to co-regulate. Opportunities should be widely made for children to make choices and decisions that consider their wishes and feelings. Early years environments should accommodate children who need time to display strong emotions, to rest, relax and be alongside skilled practitioners who can help them to co-regulate and self-calm.

Working with children in care

The term 'children in care' refers to children who are looked after by a local authority. Children removed from their parents because of abuse or neglect for a short- or long-term basis are placed with foster carers or sometimes with other family members who have been assessed and deemed suitable and appropriate to care for the child. Working with children in care requires a level of understanding and appreciation of how best to meet their needs, particularly their emotional needs given their circumstances. Early years practitioners can offer a tremendous amount of support when children who are in care attend their setting. For children accessing childcare and early education at a time of significant upset and upheaval, the consistency offered by a familiar person who knows the child and with whom there is an established relationship is crucial. This is particularly important for children who are placed in foster care and not with family or family friends who know them. Most children will at some point each week have contact or 'family time' with parents or other family members. This will be in agreement with the local authority and will take place at a time and venue chosen to best meet the child's needs. I spoke with some ex-colleagues who work with children in care and who provide opportunities for family time in their centre. Staff support children and parents to spend valuable time together whilst also assessing parent and child engagements and interactions, which inform part of a wider court process. I asked my old colleagues what the most important things were to consider for early years practitioners working with children in care and how might they be able to support children through this difficult time.

Things to consider when working with young children in care:

- Understand trauma and the benefits of working in a trauma informed context so that practitioners can meet children's needs.
- Work to de-stigmatise the child by helping them fit in without drawing attention to their difference in family circumstances. Particularly at the start and end of the day when people other than parents drop off and collect them from the setting.
- Be aware of the arrangements for family time (contact with parents), taking opportunity to be aware of and observe any changes in the child's behaviours.
- Identify support that is needed for the child, making use of the role of the key person who will notice if a child is upset or withdrawn, particularly after family time sessions with parents.
- Work closely with foster parents, other significant family members who have care of the child and social workers. If practitioners are concerned that family time is emotionally harmful for the child, they should discuss this with the child's social worker.

Life story work

It might take a long period of time before it becomes clear as to the long-term outcome for a child in care. Assessment by social care and subsequent court processes take time to complete and conclude. If a child is adopted outside of their family, records or experiences of their time in an early years setting are very important to capture and keep for them to take with them as they move on. Think about the memories that we automatically capture in photographs, artwork or special occasions such as birthdays and other important celebrations. Children in care may not have any means by which to remember these important moments. More so when they are older, they will have little evidence or recollection of memories that help them piece together their early years as difficult as they may have been. Life story books provide children in care with a record and an account of their lives pre-adoption, helping them make meaning of their situation both at the time or later when they can better understand it. Having a record of family history, photographs and associations with people who were important to them during this time is essential. Life story books will capture many things:

- Pictures of the child, where they were born, lived or where they went to nursery.
- Pictures and names of parents, grandparents, brothers and sisters, other family members or pets.
- Details of family history and places of importance including foster parents' homes and wider families.
- Explanations as to why they could not live with their parents, the reasons why they became a child in care and what it means to be adopted.

Social workers may begin gathering information to help create a child's life story book and early years practitioners will be able to provide lots of things to contribute too. Here are some helpful things to consider:

- Take lots of photographs of life in the setting and if the child is old enough invite them to take their own pictures.
- Create a record of who worked with the child, their favourite things and what they liked and disliked.
- Write a letter to the child telling them about their time in the setting that they can read when they are older. Don't be afraid to mention that this was a difficult time for them, be realistic, be hopeful!

• Talk to the social worker and/or foster parents about how you can support the child's transition into adoption.

Modelling and promoting preventative measures and interventions

Creating safe cultures in early years settings very much involve recognising the importance of putting into place preventative measures that keep children safe and well. Interventions such as following safe sleep practices, online safety measures and accident prevention strategies contribute enormously to effective safeguarding. These preventative interventions should both be modelled by example and shared with parents in the form of advice and information to help them to keep children safe at home.

Useful links to websites:

Safe sleep

The Lullaby Trust – Safer sleep for babies, Support for families (lullabytrust.org.uk)
Safe Sleep Scotland (safesleepscotland.org)

Online safety

CEOP Education: Education from the national crime agency (thinkuknow.co.uk)
Digisafe at LGfL Undressed (lgfl.net)

Accident prevention

Child Accident Prevention Trust (capt.org.uk)

Supporting staff wellbeing

Early years settings that understand the importance of staff wellbeing and are committed to supporting staff welfare create working environments that keep adults and children safe and well. A greater awareness and understanding of the need to support adult mental health has brought about welcome changes in attitudes and in the way that the children's workforce can best be supported. Early years practitioners responsible for staff and who recognise the importance of supporting mental wellbeing in so doing create cultures and working environments that safeguard children also. A workforce that recognises stressors and other contributing factors that impact upon adult health and wellbeing will understand how to support staff within their workplace, including facilitating opportunities for them to seek professional help if they need it. Staff who are experiencing poor mental health should also be given opportunities to explore appropriate deployment options if this is appropriate. This might include a change of role or responsibility for short or longer periods depending on their needs. Children's safety and wellbeing should always remain the focus of any actions taken, and children's needs prioritised over that of adults who work with them.

Key messages from chapter 7

- The culture of an early years setting is at the heart of effective or ineffective safeguarding practices.
- Cultural weaknesses work against the principles of child-centred practice.
- All allegations or concerns in relation to adults working with children must be addressed and acted upon.
- Management strategies that promote child-centred cultures include safe working practices, staff code of conduct and a focus on safeguarding through effective staff supervision.
- Early years practitioners need to understand and implement trauma informed practices in their settings. They also need to know how best to meet the needs of children who are in care of the local authority.
- Preventative measures and interventions further support good safeguarding practices in the early years.
- Understanding and supporting staff wellbeing aids safe practice and develops organisational cultures where adults and children are safe and well. Children's welfare should always be prioritised over that of any adult working with them.

Figure 7.1   Ivy's happy place on holiday with her family and cats.

References

Cambridge Dictionary. *CULTURE*. Meaning in the Cambridge English Dictionary (Accessed 16.6.22). www.dictionary.cambridge.org.

Conkbayir, M. (2021). *Early Childhood and Neuroscience. Theory, Research and Implications for Practice*, 2nd edition. London: Bloomsbury.

Department for Education. (2021). *The Statutory Framework for the Early Years Foundation Stage: Setting the Standards for Learning, Development and Care for Children from Birth to Five*. Department for Education.

Department for Education. (2022). *Keeping Children Safe in Education. Statutory Guidance for Schools and Colleges*. Department for Education.

Fullan, M. (2004). *Leading in a Culture of Change. Personal Action Guide and Workbook*. John Wiley & Sons, Jossey-Bass.

Safer Recruitment Consortium. (2022). *Guidance for Safer Working Practice for Those Working with Children and Young People in Education Settings*. Safer Recruitment Consortium.

Tickell, C. (2011). *The Early Years: Foundations for Life, Health and Learning. An Independent Report on the Early Years Foundation Stage to Her Majesty's Government*. Gov.UK.w

Wannacott, J. (2013). *Serious Case Review – In Respect of the Serious Injury of Case No. 2010–11/3*. Birmingham Safeguarding Children Board.

Final thoughts

Reflecting upon all that has been covered in the seven chapters of this book I would say that there's been much to consider and contemplate. If I have been able to achieve all my intentions when writing, you will hopefully by now have accomplished a number of things.

You will have gained a greater understanding and awareness of the historical background of early years workforce investment in safeguarding and child protection practices. A legacy upon which you are a part of and very much collectively developing. Whilst some past services and initiatives do not necessarily remain, the principles on which they were built upon do. The unequivocal drive to place children at the centre of all achievements with a clear motivation that focusses on safe and healthy outcomes is strong and enduring.

You will understand the importance of responding to concerns about a child in a timely and appropriate way, seeing this as essential when delivering and engaging in effective safeguarding and child protection practices.

You will recognise that working in partnerships with parents can lead to transformational changes that benefit children not only in the short term but potentially throughout their entire childhood. As difficult as it may be sometimes, pressing through the challenges when the potential for the positives are 'in sight' keeps us moving in the right direction.

You will appreciate that working in a multi-agency context affords children greater opportunities for their needs to be met and for them to be protected. It is clear that advances towards developing strong multi-agency practice have been negatively impacted upon due to a growing children's workforce crisis in general exacerbated by the effects of a pandemic. The role and status of early years professionals working in partnership with others seems to remain one of great concern. Much will need to be done

DOI: 10.4324/9781003137054-8

to address the discrepancies and inconsistencies that are prevalent right now. If practice and indeed practitioners' experiences are positive, we should celebrate this; if they are not, we must continue to provide challenge.

I am inspired by all that it is achieved with every early years practitioner, recognising the invaluable position and roles that you have that make significant differences in the lives of young children. For the hard work that sometimes goes unnoticed, for the tenacity to stick with it when it becomes so very demanding, for the unwavering determination to keep doing what you do, thank you to each and every one of you.

Index

Page numbers in *italics* indicate figures.

reflective practitioners and 61; training
and 64–65
compliance 54–58, 141–142
confidence 69–73
Conkbayir, M. 101–104, 181–182
contextual safeguarding 65, 99–100
Co-operating to safeguard children
(2017) 58
County Lines 93–94, 144
Covey, S. 77, *78*
COVID-19 pandemic: child abuse and
neglect during 6–7; children's social
care during 8–9; deficits in integrated
approaches during 7–8; food bank
services and 11–12; health visiting
services during 8; impact on early
childhood workforce 8–10; impact on
poor families 33, 85; impact on young
children 6–7; reduction in community-
based services during 7; social care
referrals and 8–9; unseen children
and 7, 9
Crying Shame, A 3
culture: child-centred focus and 48, 68,
166, 176, 186; defining 162; leadership
and 162–169, 185–186; open and
transparent 169; preventative measures
for safe 185; safeguarding toxins and
nutrients 163–164; staff wellbeing and
185–186; unhealthy and dangerous
165–168

directional leadership 74
disabled children: bruising protocol
for immobile 45; early help and 116;
fabricated and induced illness (FII) and
94; levels of need and 114; physical
abuse and 40; risk factors for 105
disclosure: children's lack of 119–121;
early years practitioners experiences of
121–124; recording 121, 123; reporting
121, 123–124; responding to 121–123
disguised compliance 141–142
distributed leadership 75
domestic abuse: defining 91–92;
emotional abuse and 36–38; impact

on children 92–93; Operation
Encompass initiative 138–140; parent/
carer-practitioner partnerships and
138–140; as risk factor for children
4–5, 83, 91–93, 144
Domestic Abuse Act (2021) 91

early help *see* early intervention-early
help
early help assessment 117–118
early help plan 117
early intervention-early help: background
for 114–116; child protection and
114–115; early help assessment
and 117–118; early help plan and
117; Family Help services and 119;
importance of 116; lead professional
and 117; levels of need and 113, 180;
safeguarding lead and 62; significant
harm protection and 118–119; taking
action in 117; vulnerable children and
19, 116–117
Early Intervention Foundation 104, 116
Early Years Foundation Stage (England):
disclosure in 121; early intervention
and 118; key person principles and
23; legal status of 56; practitioner
training and 64; reflective practice
and 179–181; reform of child abuse by
practitioners in 167; response to FGM
in 91; staff supervision and 180–181
early years practitioners: active
engagement 14–15; allegations of harm
and 168–178; analysis of situations
and 125–126; child abuse by 166–168;
child-centred focus and 141, 176–177;
child development expertise and
21, 34–35; child safeguarding and
protection 1, 12–16, 24–25; child's
disclosure and 119–124; code of
conduct and 177–178; decision-
making and 126–127, 130–131;
education and training 13–14; impact
of COVID-19 pandemic on 8–10;
information-sharing and 158, 160;
intuitive reasoning and 124–125; key